In This Corner

Match 1 – The Wrestlers of the Beginning

Rounds 1–6: Jacob, Abraham, Moses, Job, Ruth, Deborah

Learning to fight. Wrestling for identity, justice, calling, and place.

In This Corner: Match 1 – The Wrestlers of the Beginning

Scripture quotations marked NIV are taken from the *Holy Bible, New International Version®, NIV®*. Copyright ©1973, 1978, 1984, 2011 by Biblica, Inc.™ Used by permission. All rights reserved worldwide.

This is a work of narrative theology and creative nonfiction. While grounded in Scripture and historical context, certain elements—such as the voice of the Fighter and the Corner Man—represent imaginative reflection intended to engage the reader's personal journey and spiritual wrestling. All dialogue, unless explicitly quoted from Scripture, is original and interpretive.

Cover design, interior layout, and illustrations by LB Creations LLC
Edited by LB Creations LLC
Printed in the United States of America
ISBN: 979-8-9988622-1-2
WGAW Registration No. 2305158
Published Date: June 23, 2025
Publisher: LB Creations LLC (Independent)

For rights, permissions, or bulk orders, please contact:
lb@lbcreations.llc

Dedication

To my mother—
the one who first led me to the Lord,
taught me how to pray,
and showed me that faith is not just believed,
but lived.

To the pastors who became teachers—
who gave me permission to question,
to wrestle,
to look beyond the ink on the page
and search for the Voice behind it.

To the prayer warriors—
those faithful souls who stood with me
in light and shadow,
who lifted me when I couldn't lift myself,
whose intercession became my oxygen.

To my wife—
my breath when I had none,
my shelter when the storm would not pass,
my reason to rise and the one I ache to protect.
You are the only reason I've survived this battle so far—
and the reason I fight so fiercely to stay in it.
There are no words big enough for the weight you've carried,
but know this:
Every page bears your fingerprints.
Every line was written with your love at my back.
This book breathes because you stayed.

To the battles—
each one a refiner,

each one a turning point,
each one demanding focus, courage, and surrender.

And above all,
to the God I am not worthy of—
yet who allows someone like me
to wrestle,
to question,
to rage,
to remain—
and still be loved.

Table of Contents

Prologue
"What Came After the Map"

I wrote *Freedom Map* to survive.

I didn't know if anyone else would ever read it—or if it would even make sense to someone outside my own head. At the time, I was clawing my way back from a kind of fog I couldn't explain. A spiritual and emotional dislocation. A world that looked familiar, but didn't feel like home anymore.

That book was about finding direction again. About realizing I wasn't broken, just misaligned. It was about healing my lens—so I could see life, God, and myself clearly again. It was filled with tools, maps, prayers, and frameworks I built not as an expert, but as someone holding a cracked compass and praying it still worked.

And maybe it helped. Maybe you read it and found yourself breathing a little deeper. Seeing a little clearer. Remembering some joy that used to feel far away. I hope so. Because writing it helped me remember mine.

But the truth is: *Freedom Map* was only half the journey.

Because clarity alone doesn't remove the struggle. Sometimes it actually makes the fight sharper.

If Freedom Map was about finding my way again— This book is about what I had to do in the dark when I still couldn't see.

It's about the nights when the map didn't help. The mornings I woke up still lost. The moments I realized that even with a clearer lens, I still had to wrestle.

With God. With grief. With calling. With silence. With fear.

And what I've come to believe is this:

The wrestle isn't a sign you're failing. It's proof you're still holding on.

This book was born in those deeper places. In the sweat, the silence, the swinging. In the ring—not the retreat.

If you've ever found yourself asking hard questions, shouting prayers, or sitting in stillness wondering if God's gone quiet on you… If you've ever fought for a blessing and walked away limping… If you've ever wrestled not to win, but just to stay close…

Welcome to the struggle.

This isn't the sequel. This is the next round.

And the bell just rang.

Introduction

"You're Not Losing—You're Wrestling"

You may have picked up this book because you're tired of pretending. Tired of feeling like faith is supposed to be polished, quiet, and safe. Tired of watching others thrive in their walk with God—while you're just trying not to tap out.

If that's you, let me tell you something I wish someone had told me years ago:
You're not broken.
You're not failing.
You're not disqualified.

You're wrestling.
And you're not alone.

I used to think struggle was something to be ashamed of.
That doubt was dangerous.
That anger made me ungrateful.
That if I had to fight for my faith, it meant I didn't really have any.

But I've come to believe the opposite is true.

The people God used most—the ones who changed history—were often the ones who pushed back, broke down, spoke up, and refused to let go.
They didn't win by avoiding the struggle.
They found God inside it.

A Fight Misunderstood

Part of the problem is cultural.
Most of us inherited a Western model of faith—one that values

answers over questions, composure over emotion, and spiritual success as a straight upward line.

But the Bible wasn't written in that world.

The Scriptures come from the East—a place where relationship meant more than rules, where questions were sacred, and where struggling with God wasn't a failure, it was a kind of worship.

In that world, arguing with God wasn't rebellion—it was reverence.
Debate wasn't disrespect—it was devotion.
And wrestling wasn't weakness—it was identity.

Israel means "one who struggles with God."
That wasn't just Jacob's name. That's our inheritance.

What This Book Is (And Isn't)

This isn't a devotional.
It's not a theological textbook.
And it's definitely not a list of tidy answers.

This is a fight manual.

A raw, poetic, biblically grounded exploration of what it means to wrestle with God and stay in the ring.
Not to defeat Him—but to refuse to walk away when the night gets long.

This book will show you:

- How Jacob was blessed for wrestling

- How Ruth followed loyalty into legacy

- How Deborah stood on a hill and spoke for heaven

- And how you, too, can be honest with God without forfeiting your faith

You'll learn what it means to wrestle well.
To struggle with reverence.
To question with hope.
To fight like hell while clinging to heaven.

The Structure: Two Matches, Twelve Rounds

This is *Match One*.
It includes **Rounds 1–6**—each round centered on a biblical figure who went to battle with God.

Each round unfolds through four voices:

- **The Preacher** – narrative insight, slow and smooth

- **The Rabbi** – cultural, linguistic, and theological depth

- **The Fighter** – the raw voice of the character themselves

- **The Corner Man** – the voice of God, sacred and surprising

You can read straight through, or linger round by round.
But wherever you find yourself—don't skip the struggle.
That's where the blessing hides.

Last Thing Before the Bell

If you still picture God as someone who only wants polite prayers and spiritual discipline, let me say this as clearly as I can:

He's not afraid of your fists.
He can handle your honesty.
He's not trying to pin you down—He's trying to pull you close.

This is the God who meets us in the night, lets us grab hold, and wrestles with us until the dawn breaks.

And when the fight is over, we don't walk away disqualified.
We walk away transformed.

So take a breath.
Step into the ring.
You were made for this.

Let's begin.

Round 1

The Wrestler Who Wouldn't Let Go

Round 1: Jacob — The Wrestler Who Wouldn't Let Go

Genesis 25:19-34: The Heel and the Hunger

Genesis 25:19–34

- The prophecy of struggle in Rebekah's womb
- Jacob's birth grasping Esau's heel
- The manipulative trade of the birthright for a bowl of stew

---

Genesis 25:19–34 (NIV)

This is the account of the family line of Abraham's son Isaac.
Abraham became the father of Isaac, and Isaac was forty years old
when he married Rebekah daughter of Bethuel the Aramean from
Paddan Aram and sister of Laban the Aramean.

Isaac prayed to the Lord on behalf of his wife, because she was
childless. The Lord answered his prayer, and his wife Rebekah became
pregnant. The babies jostled each other within her, and she said, "Why
is this happening to me?" So she went to inquire of the Lord.

The Lord said to her,
"Two nations are in your womb,
and two peoples from within you will be separated;
one people will be stronger than the other,
and the older will serve the younger."

When the time came for her to give birth, there were twin boys in her
womb. The first to come out was red, and his whole body was like a
hairy garment; so they named him Esau. After this, his brother came
out, with his hand grasping Esau's heel; so he was named Jacob. Isaac
was sixty years old when Rebekah gave birth to them.

The boys grew up, and Esau became a skillful hunter, a man of the
open country, while Jacob was content to stay at home among the
tents. Isaac, who had a taste for wild game, loved Esau, but Rebekah
loved Jacob.

Round 1: Jacob — The Wrestler Who Wouldn't Let Go

Once when Jacob was cooking some stew, Esau came in from the open country, famished. He said to Jacob, "Quick, let me have some of that red stew! I'm famished!" (That is why he was also called Edom.)

Jacob replied, "First sell me your birthright."

"Look, I am about to die," Esau said. "What good is the birthright to me?"

But Jacob said, "Swear to me first." So he swore an oath to him, selling his birthright to Jacob.

Then Jacob gave Esau some bread and some lentil stew. He ate and drank, and then got up and left.
So Esau despised his birthright.

The Preacher Speaks

Genesis 25:19–34
The Heel and the Hunger

There's something sacred about origin stories. Not just the moments of birth—but the shaping. The wrestling that starts before the first breath. The fight before the name is spoken.

We're told that *Isaac prayed to the Lord on behalf of his wife, because she was childless* (v.21). That's where the fight begins—not with Jacob, but with Isaac. With a man who waits for twenty years before God answers. A man who knows what it means to be the son of a promise, but also knows what it means to wait for a promise to show up.

And then—two nations begin to wrestle in the womb.

Rebekah cries out: *"Why is this happening to me?"*
But that word in Hebrew is stronger than it sounds. It's not curiosity. It's lament. It's the voice of someone carrying turmoil in her belly, both physically and prophetically.

Round 1: Jacob — The Wrestler Who Wouldn't Let Go

And God answers: *Two nations are in your womb… one people will be stronger than the other, and the older will serve the younger* (v.23).

That's not favoritism. That's reversal. The setup for a God who delights in flipping the script. A God who does not measure by birth order or social rank.

When the boys are born, Jacob comes out second—but grasping Esau's heel. A detail too strange to ignore.
And they name him Jacob—Ya'akov—from the root *akev*, heel.
But this isn't just about anatomy. It's a picture of pursuit. Of someone grabbing what he doesn't yet have. Of someone not content to be second.

Now, let's talk about hunger.

Esau comes in from the field, famished. He smells the stew. The red stuff. *"Give me some of that red stew!"*
And Jacob—quiet, calculating, wounded—sees his chance.
"First sell me your birthright."

It sounds cruel. It *is* cruel.
But here's the hard truth: hunger reveals what we treasure.
And Esau didn't treasure what he had.
He says: *"What good is a birthright to me?"*
And in that one sentence, he trades legacy for lentils. A double portion for a single moment.

The Preacher leans in here—not to shame Esau, but to hold up a mirror.
How many of us have made that same trade?
We give up the eternal for the immediate.
We hand over identity for relief.
We sell our inheritance for the flavor of now.

And Jacob?
He walks away with more than stew. He walks away with shame.
Because the fight for identity, when it starts in deception, always leaves a scar.

This is not yet the story of the man who wrestled God.
This is the story of the boy who wrestled his brother—and didn't know who he was yet.

But the Preacher knows what's coming.
And so he tells us:
Don't rush to judge Jacob.
God isn't done.
And sometimes the ones who fight dirty are the ones who wrestle deepest—because they've been grasping since the womb.

The Rabbi Speaks

Genesis 25:19–34
The Heel and the Hunger
Story Retelling with Hebrew Insight

Come.
Come sit beside the fire while the desert winds quiet.
Let us not speak of heroes tonight—but of wounds.
Because that's where the story starts. Not in glory. Not in power.
In waiting. In barrenness. In ache.

וַיֶּעְתַּר יִצְחָק לַיהֹוָה (vayetar Yitzchak laAdonai)
Isaac pleaded with the Lord.
But not a casual prayer. The word *vayetar* suggests persistence. Deep groaning. A wrestling in the spirit.

And God responds.
But the response is not ease—it is chaos.

Round 1: Jacob — The Wrestler Who Wouldn't Let Go

"The children jostled each other within her..."

Hebrew: וַיִּתְרֹצֲצוּ הַבָּנִים בְּקִרְבָּה (vayitrotzetzu habanim bekirbah)

This verb *vayitrotzetzu* is violent.

It means to crush, to smash, to run against.

These are not gentle kicks.

This is a battlefield in the womb.

And Rivka?

She does not say, "What's happening?"

She says: *"If this is so, why am I?"*

לָמָּה זֶּה אָנֹכִי (lama zeh anochi)

Not just a question of pain—but of identity.

"Why do I exist?"

It is the voice of someone whose calling feels like a curse.

And God speaks a mystery:

Two nations... one people shall be stronger than the other... the older shall serve the younger.

This is not favoritism.

It is foreshadowing.

It is God announcing that the world's ladders will be flipped.

Then the birth:

The firstborn is red—עֵשָׂו (Esav)—from the root ע.שׂ.ה, to make or do.
A man of action. Of appetite.

The second clutches the heel.

His name is יַעֲקֹב (Ya'akov)—from עָקֵב (akev), heel, and the root ע-ק-ב, which also suggests deception or ambush.

The name is layered:

Grasper. Striver. Trickster. Shadow twin.

But before he ever lied, he reached.

Before he deceived, he desired.

This was a boy hungry to matter.

Round 1: Jacob — The Wrestler Who Wouldn't Let Go

Years pass. Esav becomes a hunter. Ya'akov dwells in tents.
But do not mistake quiet for passivity.
In the tent, Jacob is watching. Listening. Waiting.

And one day, Esav stumbles in from the field, faint with hunger.
He says: *"Let me gulp down some of that red stuff…"*
Hebrew: הַלְעִיטֵנִי נָא מִן־הָאָדֹם הָאָדֹם הַזֶּה (hale'iteni na min-ha'adom ha'adom hazeh)
It's animal language—*gulp down*, like force-feeding livestock.
He does not ask for food. He demands relief.
And he's renamed on the spot: Edom—the red one.

Jacob seizes the moment.
"Sell me your birthright."
And Esav says: *"Look, I am about to die. What use is a birthright to me?"*
Do you hear it?
He despised what was his.
The sacred for the stomach.
The future for a flash of fullness.

The Torah tells us:
וַיִּבֶז עֵשָׂו אֶת־הַבְּכֹרָה *(vayivez Esav et-habekhorah)*
Esau treated the birthright with contempt.

And this, my students, is the great tragedy:
Not that Jacob deceived.
But that Esau did not care.

As for Jacob?
He buys what was already his by prophecy—yet purchases it with shame.
Because whenever we try to grasp God's plan in our own timing, we may gain the blessing but we inherit the wound.

Round 1: Jacob — The Wrestler Who Wouldn't Let Go

Jacob's name carries the ache of his method.
He grasped.
But he will wrestle still.

The Fighter

Genesis 25:19–34 — The Heel and the Hunger

They say I was born wrestling.

They say my hand gripped his heel before I had words, before I had breath. But I remember none of that. What I remember is always coming second. Always hearing stories of the firstborn. Always watching Father's eyes light up for him. Esau.

I was the second son. The one who stayed close. The one who listened. The one who watched. Esau roamed and hunted. I stayed with the tents. But don't confuse stillness for weakness. I was listening. Learning. Planning.

Esau could tear the throat from a deer, but I could read a man's hunger.

The day he came in from the field, empty and flailing, I saw it. That look—the kind of look that trades the sacred for the immediate. I didn't force him. I didn't steal. I made an offer. A bowl for a birthright.

Some call it cunning. Some call it crooked.
But I call it surviving.

You think I didn't know what the birthright meant?
That I didn't dream of being more than second?
You think I didn't carry the prophecy in my soul, the one Mama whispered to herself—*"the older will serve the younger…"*?

No, I didn't forget. I clung to it like breath.

I know what I did.
I know it wasn't noble.
But what choice do you have when you're born behind and no one's waiting for you at the finish line?

He threw it away—like it meant nothing.
I caught it—because it meant everything.

But ever since that bowl of stew, the taste of striving never left my mouth.

That red lentil mess—it fed my belly, but it didn't fill the ache. The ache to be seen. To be chosen. To be *enough*.

They remember me for grabbing a heel.
But they forget—I was reaching for something more.

The Corner Man

Genesis 25:19–34 — The Heel and the Hunger

Easy now, son.
I saw the way you reached for him—not out of hate, but out of hunger.
You came into this world with a grip, and you haven't let go since. I've been watching.

That stew? It wasn't about soup. It was about survival.
And you knew it. You always do.

I know what the others say.
That you tricked your brother. That you schemed.
But you're not wicked, Jacob. You're just starving—for more than they know how to give.

You crave the blessing like breath in your lungs.
But hear Me: The blessing isn't stolen. It's given.
And it's not ready yet.

Round 1: Jacob — The Wrestler Who Wouldn't Let Go

You want to win now.
But you've got miles to go. Wounds to earn. Names to shed.
One day, you'll wrestle Me in the dark.
And you'll know—I never left your corner.

But for now, take this round.
Not as a triumph.
As a training.

You caught your brother off guard.
One day, you'll face yourself.
And that's the real fight, isn't it?

Eat if you must.
But know this—
I'm not preparing you for a table.
I'm preparing you for an altar.

Genesis 27:1-40: A Father's Blindness

📖 *Genesis 27:1–40*

- Isaac prepares to bless Esau
- Rebekah and Jacob's deceitful plan
- Jacob receives the blessing under false pretense
- Esau's anguish and vow of vengeance

Genesis 27:1–40 (NIV)

When Isaac was old and his eyes were so weak that he could no longer see, he called for Esau his older son and said to him, "My son."

"Here I am," he answered.

Isaac said, "I am now an old man and don't know the day of my death. Now then, get your equipment—your quiver and bow—and go out to the open country to hunt some wild game for me. Prepare me the kind of tasty food I like and bring it to me to eat, so that I may give you my blessing before I die."

Now Rebekah was listening as Isaac spoke to his son Esau. When Esau left for the open country to hunt game and bring it back, Rebekah said to her son Jacob, "Look, I overheard your father say to your brother Esau, 'Bring me some game and prepare me some tasty food to eat, so that I may give you my blessing in the presence of the Lord before I die.' Now, my son, listen carefully and do what I tell you: Go out to the flock and bring me two choice young goats, so I can prepare some tasty food for your father, just the way he likes it. Then take it to your father to eat, so that he may give you his blessing before he dies."

Jacob said to Rebekah his mother, "But my brother Esau is a hairy man while I have smooth skin. What if my father touches me? I would appear to be tricking him and would bring down a curse on myself rather than a blessing."

His mother said to him, "My son, let the curse fall on me. Just do what I say; go and get them for me."

So he went and got them and brought them to his mother, and she prepared some tasty food, just the way his father liked it. Then Rebekah took the best clothes of Esau her older son, which she had in the house, and put them on her younger son Jacob. She also covered his hands and the smooth part of his neck with the goatskins. Then she handed to her son Jacob the tasty food and the bread she had made.

He went to his father and said, "My father."

"Yes, my son," he answered. "Who is it?"

Jacob said to his father, "I am Esau your firstborn. I have done as you told me. Please sit up and eat some of my game, so that you may give me your blessing."

Isaac asked his son, "How did you find it so quickly, my son?"

"The Lord your God gave me success," he replied.

Then Isaac said to Jacob, "Come near so I can touch you, my son, to know whether you really are my son Esau or not."

Jacob went close to his father Isaac, who touched him and said, "The voice is the voice of Jacob, but the hands are the hands of Esau." He did not recognize him, for his hands were hairy like those of his brother Esau; so he proceeded to bless him. "Are you really my son Esau?" he asked.

"I am," he replied.

Then he said, "My son, bring me some of your game to eat, so that I may give you my blessing." Jacob brought it to him and he ate; and he brought some wine and he drank.

Then his father Isaac said to him, "Come here, my son, and kiss me."

So he went to him and kissed him. When Isaac caught the smell of his clothes, he blessed him and said:

"Ah, the smell of my son
is like the smell of a field
that the Lord has blessed.
May God give you heaven's dew
and earth's richness—
an abundance of grain and new wine.
May nations serve you
and peoples bow down to you.
Be lord over your brothers,
and may the sons of your mother bow down to you.
May those who curse you be cursed
and those who bless you be blessed."

After Isaac finished blessing him, and Jacob had scarcely left his father's presence, his brother Esau came in from hunting. He too prepared some tasty food and brought it to his father. Then he said to him, "My father, please sit up and eat some of my game, so that you may give me your blessing."

His father Isaac asked him, "Who are you?"

"I am your son," he answered, "your firstborn, Esau."

Isaac trembled violently and said, "Who was it, then, that hunted game and brought it to me? I ate it just before you came and I blessed him— and indeed he will be blessed!"

When Esau heard his father's words, he burst out with a loud and bitter cry and said to his father, "Bless me—me too, my father!"

But he said, "Your brother came deceitfully and took your blessing."

Esau said, "Isn't he rightly named Jacob? This is the second time he has taken advantage of me: He took my birthright, and now he's taken my blessing!" Then he asked, "Haven't you reserved any blessing for me?"

Isaac answered Esau, "I have made him lord over you and have made all his relatives his servants, and I have sustained him with grain and new wine. So what can I possibly do for you, my son?"

Esau said to his father, "Do you have only one blessing, my father? Bless me too, my father!" Then Esau wept aloud.

His father Isaac answered him,

"Your dwelling will be
away from the earth's richness,
away from the dew of heaven above.
You will live by the sword
and you will serve your brother.
But when you grow restless,
you will throw his yoke
from off your neck."

The Preacher

Genesis 27:1–40 — A Father's Blindness

There's a moment in every man's life when what he *wants* to believe and what is *true* stand toe-to-toe in the ring.
This chapter is that moment—for Isaac.

Round 1: Jacob — The Wrestler Who Wouldn't Let Go

And Jacob.
And Esau.

The father can't see.
The sons aren't seen.
And the blessing gets blurred by the ache of everyone in the room.

Isaac's eyes are dim, but that's not the real blindness here.
It's his memory—selective.
His affections—skewed.
He knows the prophecy: "The older will serve the younger."
He heard it, surely, when Rebekah carried those twins like a civil war inside her.

But Isaac wants to bless Esau anyway.
Maybe because Esau is everything Isaac once was—rugged, strong, a hunter, a man's man.
Maybe because blessing the obvious son is easier than trusting the hidden one.

So he calls Esau to prepare a meal.
And somewhere between the firepit and the field, Rebekah hears—and intervenes.
Is it deception?
Absolutely.
Is it motherly instinct?
Also yes.

Jacob hesitates. Not because he's holy.
But because he's afraid.
He doesn't say, "This is wrong."
He says, "What if I get caught?"

And still, the plan goes forward.

Round 1: Jacob — The Wrestler Who Wouldn't Let Go

Goat skins.
Cooked meat.
An imitation of manhood, tailored to fool a blind father.

And here's the tragedy that breaks this preacher's heart:
Jacob lies—yes.
But Isaac *doubts* and still proceeds.
He touches.
He hears.
He smells.
And he knows something's off.

"The voice is Jacob's, but the hands are Esau's."

Friend, how often have we done the same?
We hear truth.
But we trust the touch.
We override the inner check for the outer confirmation.

Isaac blesses Jacob.
And it works.

Because blessing, once spoken in covenant, sticks.
Even if it's tangled in manipulation.
Even if it's born in a moment of blindness.

Esau returns too late, and the grief is real.
He weeps.
He begs.
He screams, "Bless me too, Father!"

But the blessing isn't a commodity. It's a covenantal shift.
And it's already been released.

Isaac trembles—violently.
And here, maybe, he *sees* more clearly than he ever has.

Round 1: Jacob — The Wrestler Who Wouldn't Let Go

He knows what just happened isn't just trickery.
It's God, still keeping His word.

Jacob will carry the promise.
But not without scars.
Not without exile.
Not without wrestling.

And Esau?
He becomes a man fueled by bitterness.
Yet he, too, will be blessed.
Just not in the way he hoped.

That's how it goes sometimes.
The blessing is given—but not clean.
The family is chosen—but not whole.
And yet the story moves forward—because God is not afraid to write His will in the handwriting of human failure.

The Rabbi Speaks *Genesis 27:1–40 — A Father's Blindness*

Come, let us walk slowly into this story—as one who steps into a grieving house. Not everything here is clean. Not every motive is pure. But every word matters.

The Torah says:

"ויהי כי זקן ישעק ישר ועיניו כההות מראות עיניו נהה ויקרא את עשו הגדול" "When Isaac was old and his eyes were dim so that he could not see, he called Esau his older son."

In Hebrew: כההות (kahot) עיניו (einav) — "his eyes were dim"

But the Sages—but who are *the Sages*? To the Western ear, you might hear "elders," and that's not wrong. But these were not merely village wise men or tribal seniors. These were the inheritors of Moses' seat—

keepers of memory, masters of the text, interpreters of revelation. They lived not in huts, but in scrolls. Their voices echo not through shofars but through centuries of debate. They are like the Church Fathers, but midrashic. Like prophets, but scribal. Like poets, but legal. They taught us to ask not just, "What does this mean?"—but "What did it mean when Moses heard it? What will it mean when Messiah comes?"

So the Sages ask: was it only Isaac's physical sight that dimmed? Or was this a man who *chose* not to see? Not to see his younger son. Not to see the cost of favoritism. Not to see the truth of what had been spoken before the boys were even born.

"The older will serve the younger."

Rebekah remembered. Perhaps Isaac forgot. Or perhaps—like many of us—he remembered but resisted.

So the scene begins with a secret. A plan. A deception. Not a noble one. Not even a righteous one.

And yet… God will use it.

Rebekah listens. She hears the conversation and calls Jacob. She says, *"Now, my son, listen to what I command you."*

In Hebrew: קול קול בני (kol kol beni) The double repetition of "voice" and "son" is striking. She is urging him to trust her voice. Not his fear. Not his instinct.

And what is his hesitation? Not moral. Practical.

"I am smooth, and Esau is hairy. What if my father touches me? I will seem to him as a deceiver, and bring a curse upon myself."

אולי כמתעתי כמטעה (ulay kim'ta'ti kim'ta'eh) *"What if he touches me and I am seen as a deceiver?"*

Round 1: Jacob — The Wrestler Who Wouldn't Let Go

Jacob fears being *seen as* a deceiver. But the truth is, he *is* one in this moment. And yet—this is not the end of his story.

Goat skins are prepared. The meal is cooked. The son becomes the actor. And he steps into the tent of a blind father with a stolen name on his lips.

אני עשו בכורך אני (ani Esav bekhorekha) "I am Esau, your firstborn."

A lie. And yet—the moment continues. Isaac hesitates. He touches. He smells. He listens.

And then he says:

הקול קול יעקב הידים וידי עשו (hakol kol Yaakov v'hayadayim yedei Esav) "The voice is Jacob's, but the hands are Esau's."

The midrash lingers here. He *knows* something is wrong. He *hears* Jacob. But he chooses to trust what he touches.

And so—he blesses. Not because he is certain. But because he is *determined*. He *wants* Esau to receive it. Even if something inside him wavers.

When Esau returns, the veil is lifted. And Isaac trembles. Greatly.

חרדה גדולה עד מאד נגדה (charadah gedolah ad me'od nig'dalah) *"A great and exceedingly bitter trembling overcame him."*

Because he realizes: He blessed the right son—but the wrong way. God has used the broken path to still lead toward the covenant.

Esau weeps. Begs. And Isaac says, "I have made him lord over you." The blessing is not a feeling to be revoked. It is a prophetic act. A covenantal current.

And yet—even Esau is not forgotten. He is given a future. A harder one. But not erased.

So what do we make of this story? Is it deception? Yes. Is it destiny? Also yes.

This is not a chapter about moral clarity. This is a chapter about how God builds nations through crooked people.

And Jacob? He will pay a price. Exile. Loneliness. A night of wrestling that will leave him forever limping.

But in this moment, he carries the blessing. Not because he earned it. But because God saw through the skins, the lies, the blindness— and still chose him.

This, children, is not a story of saints. It is a story of a family.

And somehow, in the dim tent of a blind father, the light of a nation is born.

The Fighter

Genesis 27:1–40 — A Father's Blindness

I didn't want the blessing this way.
But I also didn't want to be forgotten.

From the moment I came out clutching his heel, the world told me:
You're behind.
Not first. Not favored. Not Esau.

My father loved the one who hunted.
The one who smelled like the fields.
The one who never had to explain himself.

Round 1: Jacob — The Wrestler Who Wouldn't Let Go

Me?
I was the quiet one in tents.
I was the shadow walking behind the name.

But my mother saw something.
She remembered the words—the prophecy that the older would serve the younger.
She believed in a fight I didn't even know I was in.

So she clothed me in lies and goat skins.
Told me to trust her voice over my fear.
And I—
I obeyed.

I walked into my father's tent, and I pretended to be someone else.

It wasn't just a costume.
It was a confession:
That I didn't think I was worthy unless I wore another's name.

He touched my hands.
He doubted my voice.
But in the end—he chose to believe the disguise.

I got the blessing.
And lost myself.

Do you know what it's like to win and still feel hollow?
To walk away with what you asked for—
but not how you hoped to receive it?

Esau wept.
Father trembled.
And I ran.

Round 1: Jacob — The Wrestler Who Wouldn't Let Go

They call me deceiver.
But that name came from what I did, not who I truly was.
Still, I carry it.
Because every name in this family comes with a fight.

And now—exile.
Distance.
A future written in ink I didn't choose.

But even so,
somewhere beneath the skins and schemes,
I wonder…

Did God bless me—because of the lie?
Or in spite of it?

All I know is, I carry the weight now.
And maybe one day,
I'll stop running.
And He'll let me wrestle for the name that's mine.

The Corner Man

Genesis 27:1–40 — A Father's Blindness

He wanted to be seen.
That's all.

Not just *blessed—beheld.*
He walked into that tent wrapped in goat skins,
but underneath,
he was just a boy trying to be loved by the one man whose voice he'd never felt settle on him.

Yes, it was deceit.
Yes, it was wrong.

Round 1: Jacob — The Wrestler Who Wouldn't Let Go

But if you saw his eyes—
if you could feel the ache he buried under every obedient nod, every
careful silence—
you might understand.

The father had gone blind.
But the blindness didn't start with the eyes.

It started when Isaac chose one son over another.
When he heard God's word and still favored the strong one.
When he tasted the meat but missed the meaning.

Rebekah remembered what God had said.
She wasn't manipulating the outcome—
she was trying to *guard the word*.
But even she, for all her conviction,
couldn't deliver that promise without wounding the boy she loved.

So the fight found Jacob.

Not with fists.
Not yet.
But with names.
With silence.
With exile.

And Jacob wore the lie like armor.
Because that's what wounded boys do.

They hide their ache behind achievement.
They pretend to be strong when they feel small.
They wear the name of someone else
just to hear a father say,
"I bless you."

Round 1: Jacob — The Wrestler Who Wouldn't Let Go

But here's what no one sees in that tent:
Even as Isaac spoke,
I was there.

I heard the lie.
I saw the trembling.
And I did not walk away.

Because grace is not reserved for those who get it right.
It runs toward the tent,
into the broken places,
and finds the one hiding in another man's name.

Jacob walked away that day with the blessing.
And the bruise.

It would take years—
a dream, a stone, a ladder, and a night of wrestling—
for him to realize he didn't have to pretend anymore.

But I never left him.
Not in the tent.
Not on the run.
Not even when the name "deceiver" clung to him like the scent of his
brother's clothes.

And one day,
I'll meet him in the dark.
And I won't call him by what he did.
I'll call him by what I always saw in him.

Israel.
Wrestler.
Son.

Genesis 28:10-22: The Ladder and the Liar

📖 *Genesis 28:10–22*

- Jacob flees toward Haran
- God meets him in a dream with a ladder to heaven
- Divine covenant is extended to Jacob *despite* his sin
- Jacob awakens with awe—but makes a conditional vow

Genesis 28:10–22 (NIV)

Jacob left Beersheba and set out for Harran. When he reached a certain place, he stopped for the night because the sun had set. Taking one of the stones there, he put it under his head and lay down to sleep.

He had a dream in which he saw a stairway resting on the earth, with its top reaching to heaven, and the angels of God were ascending and descending on it. There above it stood the Lord, and he said: "I am the Lord, the God of your father Abraham and the God of Isaac. I will give you and your descendants the land on which you are lying. Your descendants will be like the dust of the earth, and you will spread out to the west and to the east, to the north and to the south. All peoples on earth will be blessed through you and your offspring. I am with you and will watch over you wherever you go, and I will bring you back to this land. I will not leave you until I have done what I have promised you."

When Jacob awoke from his sleep, he thought, "Surely the Lord is in this place, and I was not aware of it." He was afraid and said, "How awesome is this place! This is none other than the house of God; this is the gate of heaven."

Early the next morning Jacob took the stone he had placed under his head and set it up as a pillar and poured oil on top of it. He called that place Bethel, though the city used to be called Luz.

Round 1: Jacob — The Wrestler Who Wouldn't Let Go

Then Jacob made a vow, saying, "If God will be with me and will watch over me on this journey I am taking and will give me food to eat and clothes to wear so that I return safely to my father's household, then the Lord will be my God and this stone that I have set up as a pillar will be God's house, and of all that you give me I will give you a tenth."

The Preacher

Genesis 28:10–22 — The Ladder and the Liar

He left Beersheba in silence—no tearful goodbyes, no father's hand resting on his shoulder, no mother's prayer whispered into the wind for a safe journey. Just a hurried departure, born out of fear and shame. Jacob wasn't setting off on a noble mission; he was running. A fugitive with a stolen blessing, haunted by the echo of his brother's rage. This isn't a story of a righteous man beginning a journey—it's a story of a deceiver, tangled in the fallout of his own manipulation.

He comes to a certain place—anonymous, unremarkable—the kind of place a person stumbles into when there's no strength left to choose anything better. The sun has set, and with it, perhaps a chapter of his old self. He finds a stone and lays his head down, not because it's comfortable, but because it's all he has. That stone becomes a symbol—of exhaustion, of exile, of how far he's fallen.

And then God shows up. Not when Jacob repents. Not when Jacob prays. But right there, in the dark, in the dirt, in the middle of nowhere. Grace doesn't wait for Jacob to clean up; it meets him while he's still unclean. He dreams—a stairway set upon the earth with its top reaching to heaven, angels ascending and descending. The Hebrew paints it vividly: *sullam mutzav artzah, v'rosho magi'a hashamaymah*—a ladder firmly stationed on the earth, with its head touching the heavens.

Round 1: Jacob — The Wrestler Who Wouldn't Let Go

The angels aren't descending first; they're ascending. They're already here. Heaven is not as far as Jacob thought. God's presence, long presumed to dwell in holy places, is resting right where Jacob lies— alone, afraid, and unworthy.

Then the Lord speaks. Not to accuse or condemn, but to affirm: "I am the Lord, the God of Abraham your father and the God of Isaac… I am with you. I will keep you. I will bring you back." No mention of the stolen blessing. No rebuke. Just a reiteration of covenant. A promise of presence. This is not a transactional moment—it is pure, unearned grace.

Jacob wakes with trembling realization: "Surely the Lord is in this place, and I did not know it!" In Hebrew: *achen yesh Adonai bamakom hazeh, v'anokhi lo yadati.* God was here, and I had no idea. He wasn't waiting for Jacob at the end of the journey. He was beside him from the start.

Jacob takes the stone—once a makeshift pillow—and sets it upright. He anoints it with oil and calls the place "Bethel," the house of God. It's not a temple. It's a memorial. A marker of mercy. And then, for the first time in his story, Jacob makes a vow. It's still conditional: "If God will be with me…" But even so, it's a beginning. A man used to scheming begins to hope.

This isn't his transformation. That night will come later, under a different sky with a different fight. But this is the first moment he starts to turn. The first step away from deceit and toward dependence.

So what do we say to our people?

We tell them: you are not too far, not too lost, not too stained. The ladder is already here. The God who met the liar in the desert still meets people in the middle of their messes. He still whispers promises

Round 1: Jacob — The Wrestler Who Wouldn't Let Go

over sleeping fugitives. He still turns hard stones into altars. He is still nearer than we know.

And maybe—just maybe—He's been beside you all along.

The Rabbi Speaks

Genesis 28:10–22 — The Ladder and the Liar

Come. Let me tell you a dream.

Not the kind that floats gently through the night, but the kind that grabs you by the collar and won't let go. The kind that meets you not when you are whole—but when you are running.

Jacob is not on a pilgrimage. He is fleeing. Running from his brother. Running from the tent of his father. Running from the consequences of deceit and the ache of being seen.

The Torah says:

וַיִּפְגַּע בַּמָּקוֹם *Vayifga bamakom* — "He came upon a certain place."

But the word *vayifga* (פגע) means more than arriving. It can mean to strike, to collide, to intercede. The Sages say: he didn't just come to the place—he collided with it. He stumbled into the sacred by accident. Or perhaps… the sacred collided with him.

He lays his head on stones—plural, not singular. And he dreams.

וְהִנֵּה סֻלָּם מֻצָּב אַרְצָה *V'hineh sulam mutzav artzah* — "And behold, a ladder was set upon the earth."

A ladder reaching from dirt to heaven. And messengers—*malakhim*—ascending and descending. But did you notice the order?

Ascending first.

Why? Because the messengers were already with him. Even in exile. Even in shame. Heaven does not wait for us to deserve presence.

Then—God stands above it. Or, as some translations say, beside him.

V'hineh YHWH nitzav alav. "And behold, the LORD stood over him."

God speaks—not a word of rebuke. Not a condemnation for the lie. Not a curse for the stolen blessing.

But a reaffirmation of the promise. The same covenant given to Abraham and Isaac is now given to Jacob. Even here. Especially here.

What kind of God does this? One who refuses to let identity be dictated by failure. One who shows up in the place we thought we'd escaped.

Jacob wakes, shaken. And he says:

אָכֵן יֵשׁ יְהוָה בַּמָּקוֹם הַזֶּה וְאָנֹכִי לֹא יָדָעְתִּי *Achen yesh YHWH bamakom hazeh, v'anochi lo yadati.* "Surely the LORD is in this place—and I did not know it."

And here, let us pause, because the word anochi carries weight. Jacob is not just surprised about God. He is shocked at himself. At how blind he has been.

The Sages say: This was the first moment Jacob *saw* himself clearly. Not as Esau. Not as his mother's tool. But as one known by heaven.

He takes the stone he laid on. He anoints it. He calls the place Bethel— *House of God.*

But then… he bargains. "If God will be with me… if He will give me bread… if I return in peace… then the LORD will be my God."

Round 1: Jacob — The Wrestler Who Wouldn't Let Go

A conditional vow. Some say it's immature. But the Rabbi, smiling. Because faith, like people, grows. And vows, like dreams, often begin in fear.

This is not yet the Jacob who wrestles. This is the Jacob who wakes. And realizes: He is not alone. He never was.

Children, this is the beginning of a limp. The first sting of conviction. And the first scent of mercy.

He was a liar. And yet— He was loved.

And from this night, a nation would rise between the stones and the stars.

The Fighter

Genesis 28:10–22 — The Ladder and the Lie

It wasn't a ladder. Not really.

More like a staircase—ascending into mystery, into fire, into the trembling light of a world too holy for words.

And I... I was still running.

Not toward God. Not toward blessing. Not toward some divine assignment.

I was running because of what I had done. Running with the blessing still fresh on my tongue and the lie still clinging to my skin.

I didn't stop because I was ready. I stopped because the sun had set.

And so I took a stone. A cold, lifeless, indifferent stone. And I made it a pillow. Because when you've burned bridges behind you and have nothing left ahead—you sleep on what you can find.

Round 1: Jacob — The Wrestler Who Wouldn't Let Go

But in the dark, when I was too tired to pretend, He came.

Not with fury. Not with shame. Not to scold.

With a vision. A stairway. A rising and descending that pulled my heart into a truth I didn't yet understand.

The LORD stood beside me. Me—the deceiver. The runaway. The one with goat hair still stuck to his arms.

And He spoke. "I am the God of Abraham… and of Isaac."

He didn't say Jacob. Not yet. Not here.

And maybe that was the grace of it all. That He was willing to meet me before I had a name worth repeating.

I didn't earn it. Didn't ask for it. Didn't even believe it fully.

But I woke with the words etched into my chest like fire: "I am with you."

So I took the stone. The same stone that cradled my guilt. And I stood it up. Poured oil on it. Named the place "Bethel"—House of God.

But I wasn't done bargaining. I still tried to make it conditional: "If You go with me… If You keep me… then You'll be my God."

Even in awe, I wrestled.

That was the beginning of my worship.

A man who didn't deserve the dream… Still limping from the lie… Learning to wake up with wonder instead of shame.

This is not the end of my fight. But it was the first place I realized— I wasn't fighting alone.

The Corner Man
Genesis 28:10–22 — The Ladder and the Lie

You were running again. Of course you were. When shame becomes too heavy, the legs start moving before the heart can catch its breath.

You laid your head on a rock because nothing felt soft anymore. Not home. Not family. Not even your name.

And I met you there. Not in a tent. Not in a temple. In the middle of nowhere, with nothing to your name but regret and stolen blessing.

You thought you were sleeping. But I was waking you up.

I let you see it— A ladder set on the earth, its top reaching to the heavens. Angels moving. Movement between the worlds. Connection between what you are and what I see.

You thought blessing came through performance. Through pretending. Through becoming someone else just long enough to get the words you needed.

But here, in the wilderness, with no goat skins, no mother whispering the lines, no scent of Esau, I called you blessed.

Not because you deserved it. But because I never stopped seeing you.

I stood above the ladder. Not distant. Not hidden.

And I said, "I am the Lord, the God of your father Abraham and the God of Isaac. I will give you and your descendants the land... I am with you. I will watch over you wherever you go."

You hadn't prayed. You hadn't repented. You hadn't even asked.

But still—I came.

Because grace does not wait for an invitation. It goes after the runaway.

Round 1: Jacob — The Wrestler Who Wouldn't Let Go

You woke up trembling. "Surely the Lord is in this place, and I was not aware of it." You were right. You didn't know. But I was there anyway.

Jacob, I never needed your performance. Just your presence.

You named the place Bethel. The House of God. But long before that stone stood upright, you were already becoming the house I would dwell in.

A man on the run. A dreamer with dirt on his heels. A son I was still chasing.

The ladder didn't start at heaven. It started at your feet.

Because I will always come down. Even when you don't know how to climb up.

Genesis 32:22-32 The Wrestler in the Dark

📖 *Genesis 32:22–32*

- Jacob prepares to meet Esau again
- Alone, he wrestles through the night with a mysterious man
- He is wounded—and renamed
- The fight reveals both Jacob's weakness and worth

Genesis 32:22–32 (NIV)

That night Jacob got up and took his two wives, his two female servants and his eleven sons and crossed the ford of the Jabbok. After he had sent them across the stream, he sent over all his possessions. So Jacob was left alone, and a man wrestled with him till daybreak.

When the man saw that he could not overpower him, he touched the socket of Jacob's hip so that his hip was wrenched as he wrestled with the man. Then the man said, "Let me go, for it is daybreak."

But Jacob replied, "I will not let you go unless you bless me."

The man asked him, "What is your name?"

"Jacob," he answered.

Then the man said, "Your name will no longer be Jacob, but Israel, because you have struggled with God and with humans and have overcome."

Jacob said, "Please tell me your name."

But he replied, "Why do you ask my name?" Then he blessed him there.

So Jacob called the place Peniel, saying, "It is because I saw God face to face, and yet my life was spared."

The sun rose above him as he passed Peniel, and he was limping because of his hip. Therefore to this day the Israelites do not eat the tendon attached to the socket of the hip, because the socket of Jacob's hip was touched near the tendon.

The Preacher Speaks

Genesis 32:22–32 — The Wrestler in the Dark

This is the moment we've been walking toward. No more bargaining. No more schemes. Just a man. Alone. On the edge of his past, about to face his future. The river runs cold at night, and the weight of unfinished business hangs in the air like fog. Jacob sends everyone ahead—wives, children, possessions. Everything that might remind him of what he has to lose. And then he stays behind.

"And Jacob was left alone."

He is finally without disguise. No goat skins. No stolen name. No clever plan. Just the raw, unfiltered version of himself—wounded, afraid, and not quite sure who he is anymore.

Then a man appears. The text says only, "a man wrestled with him until daybreak." No introduction. No warning. No explanation. Just struggle.

Who is this man? Is it Esau? An angel? God Himself? The Hebrew is intentionally ambiguous. Because the point isn't who the man is. It's what the fight reveals.

This is not a battle for land or livestock. This is a midnight brawl for identity.

Jacob doesn't ask to be blessed with wealth or protection. Not this time. He doesn't try to manipulate. He simply refuses to let go.

"I will not let you go unless you bless me."

Round 1: Jacob — The Wrestler Who Wouldn't Let Go

What kind of man holds on through a dislocated hip? What kind of man won't quit even when the dawn rises and pain floods his body?

Jacob has been running his whole life. From Esau. From Laban. From himself. But here, in the darkness, he holds.

And the voice asks him, "What is your name?"

This is not a casual question. It is a reckoning.

"What is your name?"

The last time he was asked that question, he said, "I am Esau." But this time, there are no masks. No pretend voices. He says, "Jacob." Heel-grabber. Deceiver. The one who takes what isn't his.

And the man says, "Your name will no longer be Jacob, but Israel, because you have struggled with God and with humans and have overcome."

He doesn't say Jacob won. He says Jacob overcame.

Not by dominating. But by staying in the fight.

This is what transformation looks like in the Kingdom. Not perfection. Persistence.

Jacob walks away limping. But that limp is the mark of a man who stayed through the night. A man who faced the truth. A man who let go of the false names and grabbed hold of grace.

God didn't bless the deception. He blessed the honesty.

And that's where the blessing still waits. In the dark. Where there are no more masks. Just the ones who refuse to let go.

The Rabbi Speaks

Round 1: Jacob — The Wrestler Who Wouldn't Let Go

Genesis 32:22–32 — The Wrestler in the Dark

Come closer. But quietly. This is holy ground.

The night is not silent. It is tense. Jacob is alone. Not just physically—but spiritually, existentially, cosmically.

He has crossed rivers. Sent his family ahead. Divided his camp. And now he waits.

But what he waits *for* is unclear. A reunion? A reckoning?

And then—the story shifts with the subtle violence of Hebrew:

\u*וַיֵּאָבֵק אִישׁ עִמּוֹ\ **וַיֵּאָבֵק אִישׁ עִמּו**עַד עֲלוֹת הַשָּׁחַר**

Vayei-avek ish imo ad alot hashachar

"And a man wrestled with him until the breaking of the dawn."

Vayei-avek. This verb appears only here in the entire Torah. It shares its root with the word for dust, **אפר** (ʿefer), calling to mind the image of two figures rolling, struggling, in the dirt.

But this was not a man. Or if he was, he was more than a man. A messenger. A mystery. A mirror.

And what kind of fight is this? No words. No weapons. Just sweat and silence and the grind of presence.

Jacob doesn't run. He doesn't plead. He holds.

Even when wounded.

\u*וַתֵּגַע בְּכַף-יְרֵכוֹ\ **וַתֵּגַע בְּכַף-יְרֵכוֹ****

Vatega b'kaf y'rekho

"And he touched the socket of Jacob's hip."

The word for "touch" here, *naga*, is gentle. Almost surgical. Not a strike. A wound precisely delivered.

Page | 50

Round 1: Jacob — The Wrestler Who Wouldn't Let Go

Because this is not a fight to destroy. It is a fight to *name*.

The being says, "Let me go, for the dawn is breaking." But Jacob says, "I will not let you go unless you bless me."

And here, the Rabbi pauses. Because this is not Jacob demanding a reward. This is Jacob asking to be *seen*.

He is tired of hiding. Of pretending. Of being Esau, or Laban, or the second son.

He wants to know who he *is*.

And so the being asks, "What is your name?" And Jacob answers: "Jacob."

And then the declaration:

לֹא יַעֲקֹב יֵאָמֵר עוֹד שִׁמְךָ, כִּי אִם-יִשְׂרָאֵל

Lo Yaakov yei'amer od shimcha, ki im Yisrael

"Your name will no longer be Jacob, but Israel."

Jacob—the heel-grabber. The deceiver. The one who always takes.

Now becomes Israel—the one who wrestles with God.

Because that's what the name means:

כִּי-שָׂרִיתָ עִם-אֱלֹהִים וְעִם-אֲנָשִׁים וַתּוּכָל

Ki sarita im Elohim v'im anashim vatoochal

"For you have wrestled with God and with men, and have prevailed."

Prevailed? Not in victory. In *endurance*. In *refusal to release*.

And as dawn breaks, Jacob is limping. He has been marked. But he has also been *named*.

Not for what he ran from. But for what he clung to.

And so we say, when we bless our sons, "May you be like Ephraim and Manasseh—" And we trace that line back through Joseph, through Jacob, through this moment when a man with a limp walked into morning light and knew who he was.

This is not just a fight. It is the night we all face when we stop trying to win and start trying to be *true*.

Come, children. The dust still rises from the riverbank. But the name is waiting.

The Fighter

Genesis 32:22–33 — The Wrestler in the Dark

I didn't plan to be alone that night. I planned every detail. Divided the people. Sent the flocks. Staggered the groups like a shield wall made of names and animals. But the truth? I was terrified.

I had come so far—but not far enough to escape myself.

It wasn't just Esau waiting on the other side of that river. It was every lie I ever told. Every stolen moment. Every shadow I had outrun since the day I grabbed his heel.

And then it found me.

I say "a man," but it wasn't a man. He came in silence. No name. No warning. Just a grip that pulled me into the dirt like I was being claimed by it.

I fought him because I didn't know what else to do. I fought him because I didn't know who he was. I fought him because, maybe, I hoped he knew who I was.

And when he touched me—not punched, not broke, just touched— I felt the hip give way.

Round 1: Jacob — The Wrestler Who Wouldn't Let Go

It should've ended there. But something in me wouldn't let go.

That's the part they never tell you about wrestling with God: Sometimes the greatest act of faith is just holding on.

He said, "Let me go, for the dawn is breaking." But dawn wasn't my rescue. It was my fear. Because once the light came, I'd have to face the world again. Face Esau. Face my family. Face the man I'd become.

So I said the only thing I knew: "I will not let You go unless You bless me."

He asked for my name. And I gave it. Not the name I stole. Not the name I hid behind. Mine. Jacob.

And He renamed me. Not because I won. But because I wouldn't let go.

He called me Israel. And I limped from that river with a blessing and a wound tied together like a scarred promise.

They say I prevailed. But I think I just stopped pretending.

I didn't walk away whole. But I walked away seen.

And that, to me, was worth the night.

The Corner Man
Genesis 32:22–32 — The Wrestler in the Dark

I was there. Not beside the river. In it.

In the dust. In the grip. In the silence between each breath.

He thought he was alone. He thought this fight was punishment. But I needed him to understand: This wasn't a fight to take him down. This was a fight to hold him up.

Round 1: Jacob — The Wrestler Who Wouldn't Let Go

I didn't come with thunder. I came in the shape of a man, a shadow, a force that could only be felt in the dark.

He needed to feel it. Not just know Me with his head, but wrestle Me with his soul.

So I let him sweat. Let him ache. Let him reach for a name that was never his to begin with.

And when the time came, I touched the place that held his strength. Not to break him. To bless him.

A limp is not a curse. It's a remembering. It's how I mark my fighters— not with trophies, but with truth.

When he said, "I won't let go until you bless me," I smiled. Because he finally stopped running. Because he finally knew what he needed.

Not a stolen birthright. Not a false name. Just Me.

And so I asked his name. Not because I didn't know it. Because he needed to say it. To own it. To surrender it.

"Jacob," he said. The grasper. The deceiver. The one who always took.

And then I gave him what he couldn't take: A new name. Israel. Wrestler. Prevailer. Son.

He limped away that morning, but he walked taller than he ever had. Because sometimes, I let you struggle just so you can see the strength that comes not from striving, but from staying.

I don't abandon my fighters in the night. I meet them in it. And I never walk away first.

Genesis 33:1-17 The Limp and the Look

📖 *Genesis 33:1–17*

- Jacob finally sees Esau
- Esau runs to embrace him—but Jacob cannot fully trust
- Instead of following his brother, Jacob detours
- He walks with a limp, forever marked by the fight

Genesis 33:1–17 (NIV)

Jacob looked up and there was Esau, coming with his four hundred men; so he divided the children among Leah, Rachel and the two female servants. He put the female servants and their children in front, Leah and her children next, and Rachel and Joseph in the rear. He himself went on ahead and bowed down to the ground seven times as he approached his brother.

But Esau ran to meet Jacob and embraced him; he threw his arms around his neck and kissed him. And they wept. Then Esau looked up and saw the women and children. "Who are these with you?" he asked.

Jacob answered, "They are the children God has graciously given your servant."

Then the female servants and their children approached and bowed down. Next, Leah and her children came and bowed down. Last of all came Joseph and Rachel, and they too bowed down.

Esau asked, "What's the meaning of all these flocks and herds I met?"

"To find favor in your eyes, my lord," he said.

But Esau said, "I already have plenty, my brother. Keep what you have for yourself."

Round 1: Jacob — The Wrestler Who Wouldn't Let Go

"No, please!" said Jacob. "If I have found favor in your eyes, accept this gift from me. For to see your face is like seeing the face of God, now that you have received me favorably. Please accept the present that was brought to you, for God has been gracious to me and I have all I need." And because Jacob insisted, Esau accepted it.

Then Esau said, "Let us be on our way; I'll accompany you."

But Jacob said to him, "My lord knows that the children are tender and that I must care for the ewes and cows that are nursing their young. If they are driven hard just one day, all the animals will die. So let my lord go on ahead of his servant, while I move along slowly at the pace of the flocks and herds before me and the pace of the children, until I come to my lord in Seir."

Esau said, "Then let me leave some of my men with you."

"But why do that?" Jacob asked. "Just let me find favor in the eyes of my lord."

So that day Esau started on his way back to Seir. Jacob, however, went to Succoth, where he built a place for himself and made shelters for his livestock. That is why the place is called Succoth.

The Preacher Speaks

Genesis 33:1–17 — The Limp and the Look

It should have been the moment of judgment. The chapter opens with Jacob seeing Esau coming. Four hundred men. It could have ended right there. Not with reconciliation—but a reckoning. A reckoning for the lie. For the stolen blessing. For the years of silence.

But then Jacob does something unexpected. He limps forward. He doesn't send messengers or hide behind the tents. He goes ahead of them all and bows. Not once. Not twice. But seven times. A posture of humility. A plea for mercy. A recognition of guilt.

And Esau—the same brother who once vowed to kill him—runs to him. He lifts his robe to do so, exposing his legs—an act considered undignified in their culture. It is the same kind of running the father in Jesus' parable would do centuries later. It is eagerness. It is mercy sprinting. It is pride undone. Esau embraces him. Falls on his neck and kisses him. And together they weep.

This is the first moment in Scripture when a human being fully forgives another. And it happens not in a court, not in a temple, but in the dust between two brothers.

Jacob, the fighter, has become Jacob, the penitent. His limp speaks louder than any apology. It shows that he's wrestled—with God, with himself, with his legacy.

He says, "To see your face is like seeing the face of God." It's one of the most radical statements in Genesis. Because the last face Jacob saw before Esau was the face in the night. The stranger. The one who blessed him. Now he looks at the man he wronged, and he sees divinity mirrored in mercy.

Forgiveness has a holy shape. It bends, not breaks. It moves toward, not away.

But even still—Jacob does not fully return. He resists Esau's invitation to travel together. He settles in a different place. The reconciliation is real. The forgiveness is true. But the consequences of the past linger.

Sometimes the limp stays. Sometimes the journey forward doesn't erase the scar.

But it redeems it.

And that, dear reader, is the message for us. Not that all relationships will be restored. But that the fight with God transforms us for every other fight we face.

Jacob doesn't win. He *becomes*.

That's the shape of grace. Not erasure. But becoming.

The Rabbi Speaks
Genesis 33:1–17 — The Limp and the Look

Come. Walk with me a moment—not in haste, but with a limp.

The kind of limp that tells you a man has wrestled through the night. Not only with God, but with the ghosts of his past. The ache in Jacob's hip is more than physical—it's the weight of an identity unraveling.

The Torah opens gently here:

וַיִּשָּׂא יַעֲקֹב עֵינָיו וַיַּרְא וְהִנֵּה עֵשָׂו בָּא וְעִמּוֹ אַרְבַּע מֵאוֹת אִישׁ

Vayisa Yaakov einav vayar, v'hineh Esav ba v'imo arba meot ish.

"Jacob looked up and saw Esau coming, and with him four hundred men."

Four hundred. Not four. Not forty. A number that, in the ancient world, spells armies and vengeance. This is not a parade. This is a confrontation.

But Jacob does not run.

He does not send more bribes or play tricks or plead for delay.

Instead, he limps forward—slow, visible, exposed.

And he bows.

Seven times.

Round 1: Jacob — The Wrestler Who Wouldn't Let Go

Why seven? The Sages teach us that seven is the number of completion, of covenant, of wholeness. Each bow an undoing. Each bow a shedding of pride. A descent into humility.

But then—something unexpected.

וַיָּרׇץ עֵשָׂו לִקְרָאתוֹ

Vayaratz Esav likrato—"Esau ran to meet him."

Yes. Ran. And the word matters. Because in the ancient Near East, a man did not run. Especially not one who held power. Running meant lifting the outer robe, exposing the legs—an act considered undignified, even shameful.

But Esau runs. He lifts his robe.

He chooses mercy over pride.

The Sages pause here and smile. They point us ahead in time, to another story, another father—one who sees his prodigal son from a distance and runs. Not because his son is clean. But because his heart is full.

Esau embraces Jacob.

וַיִּפֹּל עַל־צַוָּארָיו וַיִּשָּׁקֵהוּ וַיִּבְכּוּ

Vayipol al-tzavarev vayishakehu vayivku—"He fell on his neck, kissed him, and they wept."

The word *vayishakehu*—"he kissed him"—has dots over it in the Torah scroll. Not a typo. A deliberate scribal tradition. Some Sages say the kiss was sincere. Others say it was hesitant. Some say Esau still had rage beneath the tears.

But all agree: this moment is holy.

Round 1: Jacob — The Wrestler Who Wouldn't Let Go

Because forgiveness—like wrestling—is not clean or linear. It is messy, conflicted, real.

Jacob responds:

רְאוֹת פָּנֶיךָ כִּרְאוֹת פְּנֵי אֱלֹהִים

"To see your face is like seeing the face of God."

Why?

Because the last face Jacob saw before this was the mysterious Man in the dark.

And now, in the face of the brother he deceived, he sees something divine—not because Esau is God, but because grace has a face.

Forgiveness is not forgetting.

It is seeing a person again through new eyes.

Jacob offers gifts, but Esau declines.

Still, Jacob insists: "Please take my blessing."
And the Hebrew word there? בִּרְכָתִי (*birchati*)—"my blessing."
The very thing Jacob once stole.
Now, he offers it freely.

This is what healing looks like in Torah: not reversal, but redemption.

Still, Jacob does not follow Esau.

He bows.
He weeps.
He offers.
But he does not walk with him.

He journeys to Sukkot instead, building booths.

Some say it was fear. Others say it was wisdom.

Round 1: Jacob — The Wrestler Who Wouldn't Let Go

Because reconciliation, even when true, does not always restore full unity.

Sometimes the limp is enough.

Children, remember this:

Forgiveness may come.

Reunion may happen.

But the scars remain—holy, sacred reminders that we have struggled with God and man, and lived.

And if you look closely, even Esau bore wounds—wounds of being unloved, unchosen, misjudged.

But for one dusty moment on the road, two wounded brothers held each other.

And for that moment, the world was whole.

The Fighter

Genesis 33:1–17 — The Limp and the Look

I saw him before he saw me.

Four hundred men behind him.

No words. No armor. Just dread.

But I didn't run. Not this time.

The limp reminded me who I was now. Not the deceiver. Not the shadow. But the one who held on and wouldn't let go until I was named.

Still, I was terrified.

Round 1: Jacob — The Wrestler Who Wouldn't Let Go

What do you do when the one you wronged is stronger than you—and right?

What do you say when the thing you stole is the thing they needed most?

So I bowed. Once. Twice. Seven times.

Not because he required it. But because I did.

Each bow stripped something off of me—layers of old names, old tricks, old masks. The heel grabber. The deceiver. The exile.

By the seventh bow, I was just a man. Limping. Trying.

And then—

He ran.

Not at me. Toward me.

His robe lifted. His pride laid down.

And I braced for the blow.

But he didn't strike me.

He grabbed my neck and wept.

And I fell into it like a child.

For all my wrestling, all my cleverness, all my schemes—I never expected grace to look like this.

I looked into his face and saw what I had once seen in the dark: God.

No, not because Esau is divine. But because forgiveness is.

Round 1: Jacob — The Wrestler Who Wouldn't Let Go

Because mercy is not soft. It's violent in its own way—cutting through years of fear and bitterness.

I offered him gifts, and when he said no, I begged him to take them.

Not because I owed him.

But because I needed to give them.

I needed to say: *I am not that boy anymore.*

I called the gift my blessing—*birchati*—the very word that cursed our bond.

I gave it back. Freely. Finally.

And still… I didn't walk with him.

Maybe I should have. Maybe I couldn't.

Maybe the road to Sukkot was the only one I could take with this new limp.

Because though we embraced, I am still healing.

And some brothers only meet once in peace—then part.

But that moment…

That dusty, trembling moment…

When he held me like I wasn't a thief…

When his arms said what words never could…

That was a blessing no one could steal.

Not even me.

The Corner Man

Genesis 33:1–17 — The Limp and the Look

I was with him before the sun came up.

Before the limp.

Before the fear wrapped around his chest like iron bands.

He'd made it through the river, but the real crossing was this one.

Across the field.

Toward the face of his brother.

And I knew what he feared—what every man fears when the old wounds rise: that the past would finish what it started.

So I didn't shout instructions from a distance. I walked with him.

Step by step.

Limp by limp.

When he lined up his family—when he placed the concubines and children first, then Leah, then Rachel—he thought he was shielding them.

But I saw what he couldn't: he was still leading with fear.

Still trying to manage outcomes.

Still limping in his spirit, even after the fight.

But that's the thing about wounds—he thought they disqualified him. I knew they marked him.

He bowed once.

Round 1: Jacob — The Wrestler Who Wouldn't Let Go

Twice.

Seven times.

Each bow was an offering.

Not to Esau.

To Me.

A laying down of pride, of the persona, of the need to be right.

He didn't know I'd already softened Esau's heart.

He didn't know that mercy had already begun galloping toward him.

But I knew.

I saw the dust rise as Esau ran.

I watched Jacob brace for impact.

I felt the tension in his muscles when his brother's arms wrapped around his neck—not in violence, but in tears.

And I wept too.

Not because I doubted the moment would come.

But because the boy who once wore another man's name was finally being embraced as himself.

When he offered the gift, called it *birchati*—the blessing—I saw it for what it was:

He wasn't just returning what he'd taken.

He was saying, *I'm not who I was.*

And that's what I'd been waiting for.

Round 1: Jacob — The Wrestler Who Wouldn't Let Go

He didn't follow Esau.

He turned toward Sukkot.

That's okay.

Some roads must be walked alone—for a while.

But he knew now.

He knew I wasn't just the God of his fathers.

I was his God too.

And the limp?

That wasn't shame.

That was the mark of the night we wrestled.

The mark of a man who no longer ran from his name.

Israel.

The one who wrestled…

…and finally learned to walk.

In This Corner: Jacob — Round 1

He was slippery from the start.

Came out of the womb with fists clenched, heels in hand, already swinging at shadows that hadn't touched him yet. Jacob didn't wait for a blessing—he reached for it. Grabbed it. Tricked it. Ran with it.

But you don't get to wrestle heaven without first wrestling yourself.

And that's what this round was about.

Not a match with Esau or Laban. Not even with Isaac or the lie.

It was Jacob vs. Jacob.

The deceiver vs. the dreamer. The heel-grabber vs. the hope-holder.

And the fight went longer than he expected.

Decades of running, scheming, compensating. He kept changing locations but never quite shook the fear that he was never enough—never chosen, never safe, never truly seen.

Until one night, in the middle of nowhere, grace found him. Not in a synagogue. Not in a sermon. On the run. With a rock for a pillow and the weight of shame for a blanket.

That ladder? It wasn't a vision of escape.

It was a message: *I'm already here. Heaven touches this ground, too.*

And still—Jacob didn't change overnight.

Blessings are often given in whispers, but transformation? That takes a fight.

So God met him in the dark.

Round 1: Jacob — The Wrestler Who Wouldn't Let Go

Didn't lecture him.

Didn't smite him.

Grabbed him.

Held him.

Wrestled him.

Because some of us only learn how to be held by first resisting the arms that reach for us.

Jacob didn't win that fight. But he didn't let go either.

And that's the paradox of Round 1: his victory came not by overpowering, but by clinging.

By refusing to let go until the truth came out.

And that limp?

It was the wound that proved the blessing had landed.

When Esau embraced him, Jacob still flinched. Some pain doesn't leave easily.

But that hug wasn't just reconciliation between brothers—it was heaven reminding the limping man: *You're not who you were.*

He walked into this round wearing borrowed skins.

He walks out of it wearing a name.

Israel.

One who wrestles with God and survives.

So to the reader in your own Round 1—

Round 1: Jacob — The Wrestler Who Wouldn't Let Go

The fight may not feel clean.

You may not feel worthy.

But if you're still holding on…

If the bell hasn't rung yet…

Then maybe you're not losing.

Maybe you're just being renamed.

And in this corner stands a man who learned that even limps can lead home.

Round 2

Wrestling with Justice and Mercy

Round 2: Abraham — Wrestling with Justice and Mercy

Genesis 13:10–13 — Lot Chooses to Live Near Sodom

Genesis 13:10–13 (NIV)

Lot looked around and saw that the whole plain of the Jordan toward Zoar was well watered, like the garden of the Lord, like the land of Egypt. (This was before the Lord destroyed Sodom and Gomorrah.) So Lot chose for himself the whole plain of the Jordan and set out toward the east. The two men parted company: Abram lived in the land of Canaan, while Lot lived among the cities of the plain and pitched his tents near Sodom. Now the people of Sodom were wicked and were sinning greatly against the Lord.

The Preacher Speaks

It always starts this way—with a glance. Then a step. Then a tent.

Lot didn't move into Sodom overnight. He inched. He moved toward ease, toward profit, toward what looked like Eden but whispered like Egypt.

He thought he was choosing land. He was choosing legacy.

Scripture says the people of Sodom were wicked—but Lot set up camp anyway. And isn't that the story of us all? Wanting God's blessing, but sleeping near what breaks His heart.

Lot didn't just separate from Abram. He separated from the altar. From the promise. From the place where faith speaks louder than sight.

Abram let him go. Sometimes the hardest thing is not the conflict—but the release.

Round 2: Abraham — Wrestling with Justice and Mercy

And yet, even as Lot drew near to ruin, grace was already planning a rescue.

So let me ask you—where are your tents pitched?

Are you facing the plain or the promise? Are you drifting toward comfort, or walking toward covenant?

Because what looks like paradise may be nothing more than a prelude to fire. And what feels like delay in Canaan may be the beginning of everything God intends to bless.

Don't just look at the land.
Look at the Lord.

Genesis 13:10–13 — Story Retold, with Hebrew Nuance

Lot lifted his eyes—
וַיִּשָּׂא־לוֹט אֶת־עֵינָיו (*vayisa Lot et einav*)—
a phrase that doesn't just mean "he looked." It suggests intention. Elevation. A choosing gaze, not a passing glance. In Torah, when someone "lifts their eyes," what follows is often fateful.

And what did he see?
כִּי כֻלָּהּ מַשְׁקֶה (*ki kullah mashkeh*)—"for all of it was well-watered." But **mashkeh** is more than just "watered." It implies artificial irrigation—*man-made abundance*. Eden was watered by a river from God. This plain? Fed by human effort.

The Torah adds a haunting footnote:
"This was before the Lord destroyed Sodom and Gomorrah."
—A prophetic pause, like a shadow cast backward across the scene.

Lot chose for himself—
וַיִּבְחַר לוֹ־לוֹט (*vayivchar lo-Lot*)—he *chose for himself*, emphatically. The

doubling of "lo" (to himself) signals **self-interest**, a decision rooted in autonomy, not discernment.

He went *east*—
מִקֶּדֶם (*mikkedem*)—but this doesn't just mean a compass direction.
Mikkedem is also "from before," from the ancient presence.
To go *mikkedem* is to walk **away from sacred space**.

And then he pitched his tents:
וַיֶּאֱהַל עַד־סְדֹם (*vaye'ehal ad-Sdom*)
He didn't enter Sodom. He camped *up to* Sodom—right on the border.
Just close enough to benefit. Just far enough to still feel clean.

But the text isn't fooled:
וְאַנְשֵׁי סְדֹם רָעִים וְחַטָּאִים לַיהוָה מְאֹד (*ve'anshei Sdom ra'im ve'chatta'im laYHWH me'od*)
The men of Sodom were evil and sinners **before the LORD exceedingly**.
Not just bad people. **Wicked to the core, and bent in rebellion against heaven**.

The Rabbi Speaks

Look again, child. The Torah is whispering.

Lot lifted his eyes. But he did not lift his soul.

He saw land that could sustain his herds—but not land that could sustain his faith.

The word **mashkeh** tells you this wasn't Eden reborn. It was man-made. Fed by canals, not by rivers of mercy.

He moved *mikkedem*—not just east, but away from the Ancient One.

Round 2: Abraham — Wrestling with Justice and Mercy

He did not fall into Sodom.
He leaned into it.

So often, we are not seduced by evil.
We are **nudged by comfort**.

And he pitched his tents near Sodom. A tent is not a fortress. You think you're immune to the culture because you haven't walked through its gates. But the wind still blows. The noise still seeps in.

And the Torah? She sees right through it.

She names their sin as **me'od**—exceeding. Overflowing. Not just wicked, but willfully so.

And this is where Lot places his future.

So the question is not, *Why did Lot go?*
The question is: *What Eden have you built for yourself that was really Egypt all along?*

The Fighter Speaks: Abraham's Voice

He didn't ask me.

He didn't look back.

My nephew—my brother's boy—lifted his eyes and walked away. And I let him.

I didn't fight him.
Maybe I should've.

But how do you stop a man chasing what he calls blessing?

I saw the gleam in his eyes when he looked east. It looked like Eden, he said.
But I'd been to Egypt, and I knew better. I knew how beauty can lie.

Round 2: Abraham — Wrestling with Justice and Mercy

Still, I let him choose.

And maybe that's the fight that haunts me most—not the battles I
waged with kings, but the ones I didn't wage at all.

He set his tents near Sodom. He said he'd stay outside the city. He said
he'd be careful. He said he'd keep his faith.

But I've seen what soil can do to a man's roots.

I stayed in Canaan. Dry, quiet, unimpressive.
But that's where the altars are.

That's where I meet Him.

I've come to learn: The places God blesses don't always look like
blessing. Not at first.

Lot wanted land. I wanted legacy.
He looked for provision. I waited for a promise.

And I'll be honest—some nights, it still hurts.

I built tents, but I also built altars.
I let him go, but I never stopped watching the smoke on the horizon.

I knew what kind of city Sodom was.

And I knew God would not stay silent forever.

But I also knew this—
That when the time came for judgment,
I would fight again.

Not with sword.
Not with strategy.

But with intercession.

The Corner Man Speaks

I saw it before he did.

Lot's eyes went east. Eden, he thought. Egypt, I knew.

He was chasing green, but I could already smell the smoke.

And Abram—he let him go. Not because he didn't care. But because real love doesn't chain a man to the altar. It lets him walk… even toward fire.

You think that makes Abram passive?
You don't know what it costs to *not* interfere.

I was in his corner.

When the herdsmen quarreled, when the land couldn't hold their abundance—
when Abram said, *"If you go left, I'll go right"*—
it wasn't strategy.
It was trust.

Trust in Me.

The land of promise didn't look like much that day. Dry hills, dust, no cities, no shade.
But I was in it.

And that's the difference.

Sodom was lush, but cursed. Canaan was rugged, but blessed.

I don't judge a man by where he plants his tents.
I judge him by where he builds his altars.

So I waited.

Round 2: Abraham — Wrestling with Justice and Mercy

I watched Lot step away, pitching his dreams one stake at a time
toward destruction.
And I saw Abraham stay.
Stay humble. Stay open. Stay ready.

He didn't know it yet,
but another fight was coming.

And when it did,
I would be in his corner again.

Wrapping his wrists in faith.
Whispering mercy between rounds.
And showing him—
that sometimes the greatest punches…
are thrown in prayer.

Round 2: Abraham — Wrestling with Justice and Mercy

Genesis 18:16–33 — Abraham Intercedes for Sodom

Genesis 18:16–33 (NIV)

When the men got up to leave, they looked down toward Sodom, and Abraham walked along with them to see them on their way. Then the Lord said, "Shall I hide from Abraham what I am about to do? Abraham will surely become a great and powerful nation, and all nations on earth will be blessed through him. For I have chosen him, so that he will direct his children and his household after him to keep the way of the Lord by doing what is right and just, so that the Lord will bring about for Abraham what he has promised him."

Then the Lord said, "The outcry against Sodom and Gomorrah is so great and their sin so grievous that I will go down and see if what they have done is as bad as the outcry that has reached me. If not, I will know."

The men turned away and went toward Sodom, but Abraham remained standing before the Lord. Then Abraham approached him and said: "Will you sweep away the righteous with the wicked? What if there are fifty righteous people in the city? Will you really sweep it away and not spare the place for the sake of the fifty righteous people in it? Far be it from you to do such a thing—to kill the righteous with the wicked, treating the righteous and the wicked alike. Far be it from you! Will not the Judge of all the earth do right?"

The Lord said, "If I find fifty righteous people in the city of Sodom, I will spare the whole place for their sake."

Then Abraham spoke up again: "Now that I have been so bold as to speak to the Lord, though I am nothing but dust and ashes, what if the number of the righteous is five less than fifty? Will you destroy the whole city for lack of five people?"

"If I find forty-five there," he said, "I will not destroy it."

Round 2: Abraham — Wrestling with Justice and Mercy

Once again he spoke to him, "What if only forty are found there?"

He said, "For the sake of forty, I will not do it."

Then he said, "May the Lord not be angry, but let me speak. What if only thirty can be found there?"

He answered, "I will not do it if I find thirty there."

Abraham said, "Now that I have been so bold as to speak to the Lord, what if only twenty can be found there?"

He said, "For the sake of twenty, I will not destroy it."

Then he said, "May the Lord not be angry, but let me speak just once more. What if only ten can be found there?"

He answered, "For the sake of ten, I will not destroy it."

When the Lord had finished speaking with Abraham, he left, and Abraham returned home.

The Preacher Speaks

Genesis 18:16–33

This is one of the most staggering scenes in all of Scripture.

God—uncontainable, holy, just—pulls Abraham aside not to command, but to confide.

"Shall I hide from Abraham what I am about to do?"

That's not a question of information. It's a revelation of relationship.

This is the God who made the stars stooping low to whisper in the ear of dust.

And what follows is not just conversation—it's covenant in motion.

Round 2: Abraham — Wrestling with Justice and Mercy

"For I have known him," God says.

Not appointed. Not tolerated. **Known.**

The Hebrew is יְדַעְתִּיו (yada'tiv)—intimate, chosen, cherished.
God doesn't merely trust Abraham with the news of judgment.
He invites him into the grief of it.

And Abraham steps forward—not as a bystander, but as a priest.
He doesn't plead for escape.
He pleads for mercy.

"Will you sweep away the righteous with the wicked?"

He's not accusing. He's anchoring himself in God's own character.

"Far be it from you! Will not the Judge of all the earth do right?"

This is not arrogance. It's reverence wrapped in courage.

Abraham believes that righteousness—true righteousness—should
have **weight enough** to shield even the wicked.

So he counts down. Fifty. Forty-five. Forty. Thirty. Twenty. Ten.

And with each number, his language softens.

"Now that I have been so bold…"
"Though I am nothing but dust and ashes…"
"May the Lord not be angry…"

Abraham is not negotiating. He is **kneeling as he pleads**.

And then—he stops at ten.

He doesn't go to five. He doesn't try one more time. Why?

Because something shifts.

Round 2: Abraham — Wrestling with Justice and Mercy

Abraham senses what we often miss:
That intercession is not endless.
That prayer has a boundary—not of God's love, but of human burden.

And most of all—because **God ends the conversation**.

"For the sake of ten, I will not destroy it."

Full stop.

Then comes this line:

"When the Lord had finished speaking with Abraham, he left, and Abraham returned home."

No farewell. No wrap-up. Just silence and separation.

God had spoken all He intended to speak.
Abraham had asked all he could bear to ask.

And that's what spiritual maturity looks like sometimes:
To walk away not with all the answers, but with the trust that God heard you.

And that He will do what is right.

Abraham didn't win. He didn't lose.

He **stood in the gap**, and when the gap became too wide for a man to hold,
God stepped in, in His own way, on His own terms.

Mercy didn't save the city.

But it **did remember Lot**.

And that is enough to keep praying.

Enough to keep believing.

Enough to walk home—quiet, tired, and still in covenant.

Genesis 18:16–33 – Story Retelling with Hebrew Insight

The men rose from their meal with Abraham and turned their faces toward Sodom.

In Hebrew: וַיַּשְׁקִפוּ עַל־פְּנֵי סְדֹם (vayashkifu al-penei Sodom)—
They looked down over Sodom. But the root word שָׁקַף (sh-k-f) often implies not just a glance, but a judgmental gaze. A divine weighing.

And then God says aloud—almost to Himself—
"Shall I hide from Abraham what I am about to do?"
Hebrew: הַמְכַסֶּה אֲנִי (hamekhaseh ani)
—from the root כָּסָה (kasah), meaning to cover or conceal.

This is not just strategy. This is **God deciding whether to pull Abraham into the tension of justice**. It's the moment before revelation—before intimacy becomes burden.

He says, "For I have known him…"
Hebrew: יְדַעְתִּיו (yada'tiv)
Not chosen. Not appointed. **Known.**
This is the same word used for Adam knew Eve. It's covenantal. Relational. Vulnerable.

God explains: Abraham will become a great nation—but more than that, he must **teach his children the way of the Lord: to do righteousness and justice.**
Hebrew: צְדָקָה וּמִשְׁפָּט (tzedakah u'mishpat)
These two words are not interchangeable.

- **Tzedakah** is charity, righteousness, restorative action.

Round 2: Abraham — Wrestling with Justice and Mercy

- **Mishpat** is legal justice, equity, structure.

God is saying: "Abraham must embody both mercy and justice, just like I do."

Then comes the indictment:
"The outcry of Sodom and Gomorrah is great, and their sin is very grievous."
Hebrew: זַעֲקַת סְדֹם... כִּי־רָבָּה... כִּי־כָבְדָה מְאֹד (za'akat Sodom... ki-rabbah... ki-kavdah me'od)

- **Za'akah** is a scream. A cry of victims.

- **Kavdah me'od** means their sin was **very heavy**, a burden on the earth.

Abraham steps forward. וַיִּגַּשׁ אַבְרָהָם (vayigash Avraham)
This word "vayigash" is the same used later when Judah pleads before Joseph.
It means to draw near—not just physically, but emotionally, **willing to risk yourself** in the moment.

He asks: "Will You sweep away the righteous with the wicked?"
And here the Rabbi would point to the contrast:

- He doesn't ask, "Are there wicked men?"

- He asks: "If there are righteous ones, will You not spare the city?"

Abraham counts downward. Fifty. Forty-five. Forty. Thirty. Twenty. Ten.
Each time he begins with **an apology**, a diminishing of self:
"Now that I've dared speak..."
"Though I am dust and ashes..."

"Please don't be angry…"
These are the words of a man aware that **mercy is not cheap**.

And then—he stops.
Not because he's satisfied.
But because the next move belongs to God alone.

The Rabbi Speaks

Genesis 18:16–33

Come.
Sit with me at the edge of the oaks.
The meal has ended. The men have risen. The dust is still warm where the Presence sat.

And now—God speaks aloud. Not to command. Not to proclaim. But to wonder.

"Shall I hide from Abraham what I am about to do?"

הַמְכַסֶּה אֲנִי — Hamekhaseh ani.
To hide. To cover.

This is not God calculating justice. This is God **weighing intimacy**.

What kind of God pauses to let a human into His holy ache?
What kind of covenant shares not just blessing—but burden?

And then comes the phrase:
"For I have known him."

יְדַעְתִּיו — Yada'tiv.
Not appointed. Not employed.
Known.
Intimately. Tenderly. Like a father knows a son. Like a potter knows the curve of the clay.

Round 2: Abraham — Wrestling with Justice and Mercy

And because Abraham is known, he must now become something more than a nomad:
He must become a **witness to justice and mercy**.

צְדָקָה וּמִשְׁפָּט — Tzedakah u'mishpat.
Not just justice and righteousness.
But restorative mercy and ordered truth.

God is not asking Abraham to stop the fire.
He is inviting him to **feel the weight of intercession.**

And so, Abraham steps forward.

וַיִּגַּשׁ אַבְרָהָם — Vayigash Avraham.
The same verb used when Judah will later plead for Benjamin.
To draw near is not geography. It is **spiritual courage**.

And what does he say?

"Will You sweep away the righteous with the wicked?"

He dares to hold God to God's own character.
Not as an accuser. As a **friend who fears for both the innocent and the guilty**.

And then begins the descent.

Fifty. Forty-five. Forty. Thirty. Twenty. Ten.

This is not mathematics. This is **midrashic architecture**.

Each number echoes meaning:

- **50** – fullness (jubilee, Sinai)

- **40** – testing (flood, wilderness)

- **30** – mourning

Round 2: Abraham — Wrestling with Justice and Mercy

- **20** – accountability

- **10** – the edge of sanctity

Why ten?
Because **ten is the number of communal presence**.
Ten is a minyan. The fewest needed to carry the weight of holiness.
Below that, you don't have a city—you have **scattered fragments**.

And with each number, Abraham lowers his voice.

"Though I am dust and ashes…"
"Let not the Lord be angry…"

These are not negotiation tactics.
They are the words of a man stepping closer to flame.

And then—ten.

He doesn't ask for five.
He doesn't plead for one.

He **stops**.

Why?
Because **the Torah stops him**.

"When the Lord had finished speaking with Abraham, He left."

God ends the conversation.
Not in judgment. Not in haste.

In **holy finality**.

Abraham knew to stop because he **understood the silence**.

Go further, and you cross from mercy into presumption.

Round 2: Abraham — Wrestling with Justice and Mercy

Rashi said: "Even Noah's eight were not enough."
Abraham remembers. The flood taught him: **below ten, there is no container for grace.**

And still—he tried.

He walked the line between justice and love.

And when the heavens closed,
he did not rage.
He returned home.

Not because he had failed.
But because **the space between prayer and fire had been honored.**

And God—though He would destroy the city—
would not forget the man who stood on behalf of the unrighteous.

This, children, is the shape of intercession.
Not a shield.
A trembling hand reaching across the chasm—
asking if perhaps… mercy still has room.

The Fighter Speaks

Genesis 18:16–33

I didn't know how far I could go.

I just knew I had to go further than comfort allowed.

He said He was going to Sodom.
And I knew what that meant.

I had seen smoke like that before. Egypt. Babel. Ur.
The cities man builds when he forgets the altar.

Round 2: Abraham — Wrestling with Justice and Mercy

But Lot was there. My nephew. My shadow. My almost-son.

And so I stepped forward. Not because I was brave.
But because love makes you foolish sometimes.

I didn't have theology.
I had **hope**.

"Will you sweep away the righteous with the wicked?" I asked.

Not to accuse Him.
To remind Him.

I was trying to find the bottom of His mercy.

Fifty. Forty-five. Forty. Thirty. Twenty. Ten.

With each number, I could feel my ribs tighten.
I wasn't just fighting for a city.
I was fighting for the idea that maybe, just maybe, a handful of light
could hold back the dark.

I didn't ask about Lot.
Not directly.
I figured if there were ten, he'd be one of them.
Maybe his wife. His daughters. His house.
Maybe he had changed something. Maybe he hadn't changed at all.

But then—He stopped me.

"For the sake of ten, I will not destroy it."

That was it.

And I knew.

I wasn't being dismissed.
I was being spared.

Round 2: Abraham — Wrestling with Justice and Mercy

Because to go further…
Would've broken something I wasn't built to carry.

So He left.
And I stood there.

Not angry. Not triumphant.
Just emptied.

I had stepped into the fire line for people who never even knew my name.

And I would do it again.

Because that's what covenant means.

It doesn't stop at the altar.
It walks into the smoke.

And sometimes you plead all the way down…
and it still burns.

But He remembers.
He always remembers.

That's why I stayed on my feet.
That's why I went home slow.

Not because I lost.
But because **I stood**.

And sometimes, that's the fight.

The Corner Man Speaks

Genesis 18:16–33

He did good.

Round 2: Abraham — Wrestling with Justice and Mercy

Stood his ground. Spoke his heart. Carried the weight better than most.

Not many ask Me those kinds of questions.
Not many still believe I'm the kind of God who listens when they do.

But he did.

He drew near.
Not because he understood everything.
But because he trusted Me enough to wrestle.

Every number he offered—I listened.
Every tremble in his voice—I felt it.

He thought he was the only one pleading for Sodom.
He didn't know I'd been hearing **their cries** long before he ever lifted his eyes.

זַעֲקַת סְדֹם—the outcry of Sodom—was not from the wicked.
It was from the wounded.

I never forget cries like that.

And yet, I let Abraham speak.

Because sometimes a man needs to **hear his own compassion** to understand what he's becoming.

He stopped at ten.
People wonder why.

I'll tell you why.

Because mercy, to be real, must have boundaries.

He had walked the length of his heart.
Anything further, and it would've broken him.

Round 2: Abraham — Wrestling with Justice and Mercy

So I said what needed to be said:
"For the sake of ten, I will not destroy it."

And then I left.

Not to abandon him.
But to let him learn the holy weight of silence.

He didn't know that I was already planning to pull Lot out.
Not because Sodom deserved it.
But because Abraham **stood where no one else would stand.**

That's how intercession works.
You don't always get to see the outcome.

But heaven counts every word.

I bandaged his soul that night.
Not with answers.
But with peace.

And when the smoke began to rise,
I was still in his corner.

Just like I've always been.

Genesis 19:1–29 — The Destruction of Sodom and Gomorrah

Genesis 19:1–29 (NIV)

The two angels arrived at Sodom in the evening, and Lot was sitting in the gateway of the city. When he saw them, he got up to meet them and bowed down with his face to the ground. "My lords," he said, "please turn aside to your servant's house. You can wash your feet and spend the night and then go on your way early in the morning."

"No," they answered, "we will spend the night in the square."

But he insisted so strongly that they did go with him and entered his house. He prepared a meal for them, baking bread without yeast, and they ate.

Before they had gone to bed, all the men from every part of the city of Sodom—both young and old—surrounded the house. They called to Lot, "Where are the men who came to you tonight? Bring them out to us so that we can have sex with them."

Lot went outside to meet them and shut the door behind him and said, "No, my friends. Don't do this wicked thing. Look, I have two daughters who have never slept with a man. Let me bring them out to you, and you can do what you like with them. But don't do anything to these men, for they have come under the protection of my roof."

"Get out of our way," they replied. "This fellow came here as a foreigner, and now he wants to play the judge! We'll treat you worse than them." They kept bringing pressure on Lot and moved forward to break down the door.

But the men inside reached out and pulled Lot back into the house and shut the door. Then they struck the men who were at the door of the house, young and old, with blindness so that they could not find the door.

Round 2: Abraham — Wrestling with Justice and Mercy

The two men said to Lot, "Do you have anyone else here—sons-in-law, sons or daughters, or anyone else in the city who belongs to you? Get them out of here, because we are going to destroy this place. The outcry to the Lord against its people is so great that he has sent us to destroy it."

So Lot went out and spoke to his sons-in-law, who were pledged to marry his daughters. He said, "Hurry and get out of this place, because the Lord is about to destroy the city!" But his sons-in-law thought he was joking.

With the coming of dawn, the angels urged Lot, saying, "Hurry! Take your wife and your two daughters who are here, or you will be swept away when the city is punished."

When he hesitated, the men grasped his hand and the hands of his wife and of his two daughters and led them safely out of the city, for the Lord was merciful to them. As soon as they had brought them out, one of them said, "Flee for your lives! Don't look back, and don't stop anywhere in the plain! Flee to the mountains or you will be swept away!"

But Lot said to them, "No, my lords, please! Your servant has found favor in your eyes, and you have shown great kindness to me in sparing my life. But I can't flee to the mountains; this disaster will overtake me, and I'll die. Look, here is a town near enough to run to, and it is small. Let me flee to it—it is very small, isn't it? Then my life will be spared."

He said to him, "Very well, I will grant this request too; I will not overthrow the town you speak of. But flee there quickly, because I cannot do anything until you reach it." (That is why the town was called Zoar.)

By the time Lot reached Zoar, the sun had risen over the land. Then the Lord rained down burning sulfur on Sodom and Gomorrah—from the Lord out of the heavens. Thus he overthrew those cities and the entire plain, destroying all those living in the cities—and also the vegetation in the land.

But Lot's wife looked back, and she became a pillar of salt.

Early the next morning Abraham got up and returned to the place where he had stood before the Lord. He looked down toward Sodom and Gomorrah, toward all the land of the plain, and he saw dense smoke rising from the land, like smoke from a furnace.

So when God destroyed the cities of the plain, he remembered Abraham, and he brought Lot out of the catastrophe that overthrew the cities where Lot had lived.

The Preacher Speaks

Genesis 19:1–29

This is not a story for the faint of heart.

The angels arrive at Sodom in the evening. That's no accident. Evening is when shadows lengthen. When it's harder to tell what's righteous and what's just familiar.

And Lot is waiting.

Not the same Lot who journeyed with Abraham.
This one is older. Tired. Rooted in the wrong soil too long.

He greets the messengers, bows low, and urges them to come under his roof.
Hospitality, yes. But also desperation.
Because he knows this city. He knows what comes after dark.

Round 2: Abraham — Wrestling with Justice and Mercy

They decline at first. "We'll spend the night in the square," they say.
But Lot presses them—strongly.
Not out of kindness, but out of fear.

And the fear proves true.

The men of Sodom come, "from every part of the city—both young and old."
That phrase matters.
This isn't isolated wickedness.
It's cultural rot. Generational. Systemic.

And then Lot offers the unthinkable:
"Don't do this to my guests… take my daughters instead."

This is where the reader recoils.
Rightly so.

Because what Lot offers is not righteousness.
It's survival.

He has lived in this city too long.
The boundaries are blurry. The instinct to protect is corrupted.

But the angels intervene.
They pull Lot back inside and strike the mob blind.

That image alone tells you what kind of God we're dealing with:
One who will not let even a compromised man face judgment alone.

The messengers ask, "Is there anyone else here? Sons-in-law? Daughters?"

Lot runs to his future sons-in-law and begs them to leave.
But they laugh. They think he's joking.

How do you warn people who've grown numb to sin?

Round 2: Abraham — Wrestling with Justice and Mercy

The next morning, Lot still hesitates.
And the angels take him by the hand—him, his wife, his daughters—
and lead them out.

Why?
Not because of Lot's righteousness.
But because of Abraham's intercession.

That's what verse 29 says:
"God remembered Abraham, and He brought Lot out…"

God did not forget the man who stood in the gap.
Even when the city burned.

Lot is told not to look back. But his wife does.
And she turns to salt.

Why?
Not as punishment.
But as exposure.

She didn't flee with her whole heart.
Her body moved, but her soul stayed behind.

You can't be rescued halfway.
You can't run from destruction while grieving its absence.

And Abraham?
He rises early.
He stands in the place where he once stood before God.

And he sees it:
The smoke.
The judgment.
The silence.

Round 2: Abraham — Wrestling with Justice and Mercy

He doesn't gloat.
He doesn't celebrate.

He watches.

Because when you've prayed like that—
When you've stood in the holy place and begged for mercy—
You don't walk away untouched.

And when you see the smoke rising...
You don't say, "They got what they deserved."

You say,
"Lord, remember the righteous. Even if it's just one."

And friend—if you're wondering what all this means for you—let me say this plainly:

God didn't rescue Lot because Lot was righteous.
He rescued Lot because someone interceded.

Someone stood in the tension between justice and mercy and refused to walk away.

That matters.

Your prayers matter.
Your presence in someone else's mess matters.

You might be the only reason mercy gets into the city at all.

And when it does?
Sometimes it doesn't look like victory.
Sometimes it looks like barely getting out, eyes red, heart aching, asking if it was enough.

But you stood.
And heaven remembers.

Round 2: Abraham — Wrestling with Justice and Mercy

And if you've ever stood in the gap for someone walking toward fire—
If you've ever prayed all the way down and still watched the smoke rise—

Then you know what it means to battle God,
and walk away with a limp.

Because love will mark you.

And blessing?
Blessing doesn't always look like fireproof skin.

Sometimes it looks like staying faithful when your prayers don't seem to work.

But one day, another Intercessor stood outside another city—
and He didn't stop at ten.

He became the One.

And in Him, judgment and mercy finally kissed.

Genesis 19:1–29 – Story Retelling with Hebrew Insight

Two messengers arrive in Sodom just as the day folds into dusk.
וַיָּבֹאוּ שְׁנֵי הַמַּלְאָכִים סְדֹמָה בָּעֶרֶב (vayyavo'u shnei ha-malachim Sedomah ba-erev)
"Ba-erev" means *evening*, but its root (ע-ר-ב) also means *mixture* or *ambiguity*. It's the hour when boundaries blur.
Light is fading. Clarity is gone. Shadows stretch long across compromised ground.

Lot is waiting—not outside the camp like Abraham, but inside the gate of the city.
בְּשַׁעַר סְדֹם (b'sha'ar Sedom)
The gate is where judgments are made and status is shown. Lot has climbed the civic ladder—but at what cost?

Round 2: Abraham — Wrestling with Justice and Mercy

He bows low. He urges them to come to his home.
וַיִּפְצַר-בָּם מְאֹד (vayyiftzar bam me'od)
He insists strongly. The word *patsar* suggests pleading that borders on desperation. He knows what Sodom becomes after dark.

Inside, he prepares a feast.
וּמַצּוֹת אָפָה (umatztot afah) — unleavened bread.
This echoes the haste of Exodus. A meal made in urgency. A deliverance prefigured.

But outside, the city gathers.
מִנַּעַר וְעַד-זָקֵן ... כָּל הָעָם מִקָּצֶה (mina'ar v'ad zaken... kol ha'am miqatzeh)
From youth to elder, all the people, from every quarter.
This is not isolated sin. It is systemic depravity. Generational corruption. The city stands as one, unified in violation.

"Where are the men who came to you tonight? Bring them out to us so that we may know them."
וְנֵדְעָה אוֹתָם (v'ned'ah otam)

The word *yada*—"to know"—echoes the language of covenant. It is the same word used for "Adam knew Eve."
But here? It is weaponized.
This is not knowing as intimacy.
This is knowing as conquest. As desecration.

They want the holy unmade.
They want to degrade the divine visitors.
They seek to violate the image of God in order to assert their own power.

Lot steps outside.
He closes the door behind him.
He stands alone in the breach.

And then—he speaks words that chill the bones:

Round 2: Abraham — Wrestling with Justice and Mercy

"Look, I have two daughters who have never known a man. Let me bring them out to you…"

No commentary can explain this away.

וְאַל-תַּעֲשׂוּ דָבָר לָאֲנָשִׁים הָאֵל (v'al ta'asu davar la'anashim ha'eleh)
"Do nothing to these men…"

Lot is protecting the sacred at the expense of the innocent.

Why?

Because the Sodomite culture has seeped into him.
Because his moral compass, though once directed by Abraham, has been dulled.
Because even his idea of righteousness has become transactional.

This is not Abraham's intercession.
This is not courage.
This is the trembling calculus of a man shaped by compromise.

But even here—God acts.

The mob rejects Lot's offer. They surge forward.
Then the messengers intervene—pulling Lot in and shutting the door.

They strike the mob with סַנְוֵרִים (sanverim) — a rare word for blindness.
Used only once more in 2 Kings 6, it implies more than physical blindness.
It is *madness. Disorientation. A fog of judgment.*
They grope for the door but cannot find it.
Not because they cannot see—but because they cannot discern.

The angels say: *It's time.*

"Whom else do you have here? Sons-in-law? Daughters?"
"Get them out of this place…"

Round 2: Abraham — Wrestling with Justice and Mercy

Lot warns his sons-in-law, but they mock him.
וַיְהִי כִמְצַחֵק (vayehi kimetzachek)
Like one who jokes. The root צ־ח־ק (laugh) is used here in contempt.
It is the same root that names Isaac—but here it is hollow.
They laugh not in joy, but in scorn.
They cannot fathom that judgment is real.

Dawn breaks.
But Lot lingers.

And then, mercy takes hold.

וַיַּחֲזִקוּ הָאֲנָשִׁים בְּיָדוֹ... כִּי חָמַל יְהוָה עָלָיו (vayachaziku ha-anashim b'yado...
ki ḥamal YHWH alav)
"They seized his hand... for the LORD had compassion on him."
חָזַק (ḥ-z-k) — to grasp with strength.
חָמַל (ḥ-m-l) — to spare, to show mercy.
Lot is not saved by wisdom. He is dragged out by grace.

"Flee for your lives! Don't look back!"

But Lot pleads again—this time for a smaller escape.
מִצְעָר הִוא (mitz'ar hi) — "It is small."
He bargains not for righteousness, but for *comfort.*
Even now, he is more Sodomite than pilgrim.

He reaches Zoar as the sun rises.
כְּצֵאת הַשֶּׁמֶשׁ עַל-הָאָרֶץ (ketzeit ha-shemesh al ha-aretz)
The light splits judgment from mercy.

Then it comes.

וַיהוָה הִמְטִיר עַל-סְדֹם וְעַל-עֲמֹרָה גָּפְרִית וָאֵשׁ (v'YHWH himtir al Sedom v'al
Amora gophrith va'esh)
"God rained down sulfur and fire."
Himtir—the same verb used when He once rained manna.
Now He rains down wrath.

Round 2: Abraham — Wrestling with Justice and Mercy

Abraham rises early.
He returns to הַמָּקוֹם (ha-makom)—"the place."
But also, *The Omnipresent One.*

He sees smoke rising.

וְהִנֵּה עָלָה קִיטֹר הָאָרֶץ (v'hinei alah qitor ha-aretz)
"Behold, the smoke of the land went up like the smoke of a furnace."
Not the fire of Sinai.
But the fire of forfeited covenant.

The Rabbi Speaks

Genesis 19:1–29

Come close, child. This part of the story is not told lightly. We have left the oaks. The meal has ended. The covenant has been spoken. But now, we journey with the messengers into the city—a city where the outcry has reached the heavens, and the silence of the righteous is deafening.

Evening falls. The messengers arrive in Sodom just as the last threads of light unravel. In Hebrew, the word for evening is ערב (erev)—a word that does not merely mean nightfall, but mingling, confusion, a time when distinctions blur. Shadows stretch across the stone streets. And standing at the gate is Lot.

Yes, that Lot. Abraham's nephew. A man who once followed blessing but now sits inside the very place from which the blessing flees. He sees the strangers. He knows. He bows. He pleads.

וַיִּפְצַר בָּם מְאֹד (vayyiftzar bam me'od) He urged them strongly. Desperately. As if his soul recognized the peril his city carried on its breath.

Round 2: Abraham — Wrestling with Justice and Mercy

They enter. He bakes them matzot—unleavened bread. The same symbol of haste that will one day appear in Egypt. Even here, deliverance is rehearsed.

But the city does not rest. They come. Not a handful. Not a mob. But everyone.

מִנַּעַר וְעַד-זָקֵן כָּל-הָעָם מִקָּצֶה (mina'ar v'ad zaken, kol ha'am miqatzeh) From the youngest to the oldest, from every edge of the city, they encircle Lot's house. This is not individual sin. This is structural decay. A society with no compass.

They demand the visitors. "Bring them out to us so that we may know them."

נֵדְעָה אֹתָם (ned'ah otam) Yada—to know. A word that once described Adam and Eve's sacred union. A word that denotes intimacy, covenant, vulnerability. But here? It is twisted. In Sodom, even the language of knowing has been corrupted into violence.

And then—Lot. He steps outside. He closes the door behind him.

וַיִּגַשׁ נַעֲוֹתָם (vayyigash na'alem) He draws near. This same verb will later describe Judah as he pleads before Joseph. But this is not Judah. This is Lot. And what he says next chills even the prophets:

"Look, I have two daughters... Let me bring them out to you."

The Torah does not pause to explain. And neither should we. Lot does not offer his daughters because he is righteous. He offers them because he has lived too long in Sodom. Because compromise has worn grooves into his soul. Because when you live in a place long enough, the unthinkable becomes thinkable.

This is not courage. This is not protection. This is survival warped by fear.

Round 2: Abraham — Wrestling with Justice and Mercy

And still, mercy intervenes.

The messengers reach through the door. They pull Lot inside. They shut out the darkness.

וְאֶת-הָאֲנָשִׁים בְּסַנְוֵרִים (v'et ha'anashim b'sanverim) They strike the men outside with blindness. But not just physical. The word sanverim appears only twice in the Tanakh. It means disorientation, madness, divine confusion. They grope for the door, but they cannot find it. Not because their eyes are shut, but because their hearts are sealed.

Morning comes. And Lot still hesitates.

And so the messengers seize his hand.

וַיַּחֲזִקוּ בְיָדוֹ... כִּי חָמַל יהוה עָלָיו (vayyachaziku b'yado... ki ḥamal YHWH alav) They take hold of him. Because God had compassion. Not because Lot earned it. Because grace does not always wait for us to understand.

Then fire. Sulfur. Smoke.

וַיהוה הִמְטִיר עַל-סְדֹם... גָּפְרִית וָאֵשׁ (v'YHWH himtir al Sedom... gofrit va'esh) God rained down judgment. Not in rage. But in resolve.

And Abraham—he returns to the place. HaMakom. The same place he once stood to intercede. The same place he waited on the Lord. And now, he sees the smoke rising like a furnace.

Not because he failed. But because the line between mercy and rot had been walked.

And still—Lot was spared. Not for his decisions. But because the mercy of heaven sometimes comes with a grip that drags us out while we're still clinging to the doorframe.

Round 2: Abraham — Wrestling with Justice and Mercy

So remember, child: This story does not ask for comfort. It asks for reverence. Because sometimes God saves the undeserving, And sometimes, fire falls where laughter once echoed.

And still—the covenant holds. Still, the hand reaches. Still, there is a path to the mountain. Even after Sodom. Even after smoke. Even after we've lived too long in the wrong gate.

The Fighter Speaks

Genesis 19:1–29

I could smell the smoke before I saw it.

Not the fire of offerings—not the kind that rises sweet before the face of God. No, this was the kind that clings to the skin and seeps into memory. The kind that smells like judgment.

I stood where I had pleaded. The dust where I fell to my knees had already cooled.

Ten. That was the number I stopped on. Not because I was out of arguments. Not because I stopped caring. But because something in the silence told me the rest was not mine to carry.

And then the sky cracked. Not with thunder. But with fire.

I had asked for mercy. I had bargained like a father would for his child. But mercy—real mercy—does not always look like rescue. Sometimes it looks like dragging a man out of a city while he screams to go back.

That's what they told me, anyway. The messengers. That's what happened to Lot.

Lot. He was never wicked. But he wasn't whole either. He thought he could live close to the edge and not fall in. He thought a tent near Sodom was the same as a life in covenant.

Round 2: Abraham — Wrestling with Justice and Mercy

I should've warned him harder. I should've pulled him back when the valley looked like Eden. But I let him go. I let him choose.

Maybe that's the fight I regret the most—the one I didn't have.

And now, the valley is ash.

I saw it. The smoke rising like a kiln. And I knew— this wasn't a failure of prayer. This was the price of rot.

There are days I still hear the cries in the wind. Not of the wicked. But of the daughters. Of a wife turned to salt. Of a man who hesitated and had to be dragged.

And yet... God remembered.

He remembered the prayer of a man who dared to step into the ring with Him. He remembered the trembling voice that counted down from fifty. He remembered me.

So I carry that. The ache. The ash. The silence after the tenth plea. I carry it like a limp.

Not because I lost. But because I stood.

And when you wrestle with God for the sake of another, and walk away with only the smoke and silence to show for it, remember:

Sometimes the mercy is in the trying. Sometimes, the prayer is the rescue. And sometimes— The only way to fight for someone is to let God finish the round.

The Corner Man

Genesis 19:1–29

Round 2: Abraham — Wrestling with Justice and Mercy

You don't always hear Me in the thunder. Sometimes I whisper through hesitation. Sometimes I stand behind you, silent, as you bargain your heart out in the dark.

You asked Me to spare them. You counted down with tears in your throat. You dared to draw near. I heard every number. I honored every plea.

But there comes a moment in every match when the corner has to be quiet. When the fighter must finish the round. And sometimes, when the flames are already lit, the mercy isn't in stopping the fire. It's in pulling one man out.

Lot made it. But not because of his wisdom. He was reluctant. Bound to a place that never knew his name. He waited too long. He offered too much. And still—I reached for him. I grabbed his hand.

Not because of who he was. But because of who you were. Because you stood in the gap. Because you dared to wrestle.

You didn't see the rescue, but it happened. Even the daughters. Even the dragging.

And yes, the city burned. But so did the corruption. So did the cries that reached My courts.

You thought ten would be enough. You hoped. And when you stopped counting, you were not dismissed. You were released.

The smoke you saw that morning wasn't the sign of your failure. It was the seal of justice and the echo of mercy. It was the sign that heaven had not ignored the voice of a man willing to pray like a prophet and fight like a father.

You walked away limping. But you walked away with Me. And long after the ashes settle, I still speak your name with honor.

Round 2: Abraham — Wrestling with Justice and Mercy

You don't always hear Me in the thunder. But I am in your corner.
Even when the fire falls.

Round 2: Abraham — Wrestling with Justice and Mercy

In This Corner: Abraham – Round 2

The Ringside Analyst Speaks

He didn't throw fists.
He didn't lift a sword.
But don't be fooled—Abraham just went twelve rounds with the
Living God.
Not to conquer Him.
To intercede. To stand in the smoke between fire and flesh.
To beg mercy for people who wouldn't have done the same for him.

He walked into this fight with a name.
He walked out with a limp on his soul.

You want to know what kind of fighter Abraham was?

He wasn't fighting against God.
He was fighting alongside Him.
Trying to pull mercy a few inches further than justice said it could go.

He counted backward—not from confidence, but from compassion.
Fifty. Forty-five. Forty. Thirty. Twenty. Ten.
And when he hit ten—he stopped.
Not because he gave up.
But because he heard the silence.

That's when you know a fighter's grown up—
Not when he can take the hits,
But when he knows when to lower his hands and say,
"This round isn't mine to finish."

The next morning, he looked out and saw what every intercessor
fears—
The smoke.

Round 2: Abraham — Wrestling with Justice and Mercy

The fallout.
The silence of unanswered prayer.

But listen to me now:

The fire fell—but Lot got out.
That rescue wasn't strategy.
It was mercy on Abraham's breath.

So don't tell me prayer is passive.
Don't tell me pleading is weakness.
I watched a man fight with nothing but his voice,
and God listened long enough to count every syllable.

That's Round 4.
And in this corner—we honor the fighter who doesn't just wrestle God for himself,
but for someone else.

Round 3

The Fight for Calling

Exodus 2:11-25 The Fugitive's Fire

Exodus 2:11–25

- Moses kills the Egyptian and flees to Midian

- He sits by a well, marries Zipporah, and tends sheep

- Israel groans in slavery—and God remembers the covenant

Exodus 2:11–25 (NIV)

One day, after Moses had grown up, he went out to where his own people were and watched them at their hard labor. He saw an Egyptian beating a Hebrew, one of his own people. Looking this way and that and seeing no one, he killed the Egyptian and hid him in the sand.

The next day he went out and saw two Hebrews fighting. He asked the one in the wrong, "Why are you hitting your fellow Hebrew?"

The man said, "Who made you ruler and judge over us? Are you thinking of killing me as you killed the Egyptian?"

Then Moses was afraid and thought, "What I did must have become known."

When Pharaoh heard of this, he tried to kill Moses, but Moses fled from Pharaoh and went to live in Midian, where he sat down by a well.

Now a priest of Midian had seven daughters, and they came to draw water and fill the troughs to water their father's flock. Some shepherds came along and drove them away, but Moses got up and came to their rescue and watered their flock.

When the girls returned to Reuel their father, he asked them, "Why have you returned so early today?"

They answered, "An Egyptian rescued us from the shepherds. He even drew water for us and watered the flock."

"And where is he?" Reuel asked his daughters. "Why did you leave him? Invite him to have something to eat."

Moses agreed to stay with the man, who gave his daughter Zipporah to Moses in marriage. Zipporah gave birth to a son, and Moses named him Gershom, saying, "I have become a foreigner in a foreign land."

During that long period, the king of Egypt died. The Israelites groaned in their slavery and cried out, and their cry for help because of their slavery went up to God. God heard their groaning and he remembered his covenant with Abraham, with Isaac and with Jacob. So God looked on the Israelites and was concerned about them.

The Preacher Speaks

He looked both ways before he buried the body. That's how the story begins. Not with a sermon, but with a murder.
Not with a command, but with a cover-up.
Not with "Here I am," but with "What have I done?"

This is not the Moses from Sunday School murals—the staff-raising, sea-parting, law-carrying legend.
This is the Moses with blood on his hands and dust in his mouth.
The fugitive. The misfit. The man caught between a calling and a crime.

He saw injustice.
He intervened.
And it cost him everything.

That's how calling sometimes begins.

Round 3: Moses — The Fight for Calling

Not with clarity—but with collision.
Not with a sense of direction—but with a spiritual nosebleed.
You step in to make something right… and end up running for your life.

He sits by a well now.
In a foreign land.
With the name of a dead man whispering behind him and the cry of a nation rising in the background.

He didn't ask for this.
He didn't volunteer.
He simply saw something he couldn't ignore—and he moved.

But now he's in Midian, and Egypt is far behind.
And whatever fire burned in him that day?
It's buried too. Somewhere beneath the sand.

Maybe you've been there.

Maybe you've stepped into the fight too soon.
Or with the wrong weapon.
Or from the wrong place in your heart.

And now you sit by your own well—wondering if the fight disqualified you.
Wondering if you blew it before it even began.
Wondering if the calling was ever really yours… or just a flare of youthful rage wrapped in a justice complex.

But here's the thing about Moses.
God doesn't cancel him.

Round 3: Moses — The Fight for Calling

God doesn't say, *"Too violent. Too messy. Too broken."*
Instead, God waits.

And listens.
And remembers.

Because while Moses is running from his past…
Heaven is preparing to call his name.

The Rabbi Speaks

(Exodus 2:11–25 — The Fugitive's Fire)

Come.
Sit beside me, here at the well. The sand is still warm with yesterday's heat, and the air carries silence—the kind that comes after failure.
But before you rush past it, let me show you something Western eyes might miss.

You think this is a story about anger.
Or about justice.
Or about running from responsibility.

But what if it's about something deeper?
What if this is the moment when the fire of God first flickers in a man who doesn't know what to do with it?

The text says Moses "went out to his brothers" (וַיֵּצֵא אֶל־אֶחָיו — *vayetze el echav*).
Not "his people," as your English translation might soften it.
No—*his brothers.*

You see, Moses wasn't just wandering among slaves.
He was stepping into a forgotten identity.

Round 3: Moses — The Fight for Calling

Raised in the palace, dressed in Egyptian linen, fed from Pharaoh's table—but something in him still burned for *his brothers*.

This isn't just empathy.
It's *recognition*.

And then...
He sees.

The word used is וַיַּרְא (*vayar*), which means "he saw," yes—but in Hebrew, to see is more than to look.
To *ra'ah* is to perceive, to understand, to *enter* into the sight.

He saw an Egyptian beating a Hebrew.
He looked this way and that.
He struck down the Egyptian and hid him in the sand.

You might judge him for the violence.
But can we ask a different question?

What does it mean when a prince raised in privilege risks everything—*everything*—for people he barely knows?

Later, when he tries to break up a fight between two Hebrews, one turns and says:

"Who made you a ruler and a judge over us?"
"מִי שָׂמְךָ לְאִישׁ שַׂר וְשֹׁפֵט עָלֵינוּ?"
(Mi samkha le'ish sar v'shofet aleinu?)

This is more than sarcasm.
It's prophetic.

Round 3: Moses — The Fight for Calling

They don't realize it yet—but Moses *will* be made ruler and judge.
Not by himself.
Not by Pharaoh.
By the God of their fathers.

The question that wounds him is the very identity that will one day define him.

So Moses runs.
To Midian.
To obscurity.
To exile.

But here's where I want you to lean in.
The Torah tells us:

"And he sat down by a well."
וַיֵּשֶׁב עַל־הַבְּאֵר (*vayeshev al-habe'er*)

He doesn't keep walking.
He doesn't pace or plan or pray.

He sits.

That Hebrew word *vayeshev*—"he settled"—is the same root used when Abraham *dwelt* in Canaan, or when Jacob *settled* in the land of his fathers.
It's not a casual rest.

It's a quiet surrender.

And then, the shepherds arrive.
And the daughters.

And the priest.
And the wedding.

And Moses says something strange when his son is born:

"I have become a foreigner in a foreign land."
גֵּר הָיִיתִי בְּאֶרֶץ נָכְרִיָּה (*ger hayiti b'eretz nokhriya*)

That word *ger*—foreigner, sojourner—is more than displacement.
It's a spiritual word in Hebrew.
It means: *I do not belong here. But I am learning to dwell here anyway.*

It's the same word Israel will use in the wilderness.
The same word the Torah uses to describe you, if you seek God in exile.

So maybe the question isn't, "Why did Moses kill?"
Maybe the question is, "What does God do with a man who's passionate… but unformed?"

And the answer?
He gives him time.
Time to sit.
Time to heal.
Time to tend sheep, not nations.
Because in God's economy, the wilderness is not punishment.
It's preparation.

Now, student—do you see?

This fire did not begin at the bush.
It began here.
With a buried body.
And a heart that could not look away.

Round 3: Moses — The Fight for Calling

The Fighter Speaks

I didn't mean to kill him.

I need you to know that.
It wasn't the plan.
I didn't wake up that morning thinking I'd bury a man in the sand.

I just… snapped.

I saw the whip.
I saw the blood.
And something rose up in me that I couldn't push down.

I've seen enough violence for two lifetimes.
But that day—maybe for the first time—I believed I was supposed to stop it.

And now?

I'm alone.
Again.

They called me a murderer.
But I thought I was stepping in.
I thought I was defending my brothers.
Turns out, they don't even want me.

"Who made you ruler and judge?"

That question cut deeper than the blade I buried in that Egyptian.

Because I don't know.
I don't know who made me anything.
I don't know where I belong.

Round 3: Moses — The Fight for Calling

I'm not Egyptian enough for the palace.
I'm not Hebrew enough for the slaves.

I'm a man with no place to stand… and blood on his hands.

So I ran.
Because it's what I've always done.
Smile when I should speak.
Hide when I should help.
Run when it all comes crashing down.

Midian is far.
And quiet.

There's no empire here.
No pyramids.
Just wells.
And sheep.
And silence.

And sometimes… I think maybe this is all I'll ever be.
A foreigner.
A mistake.
A man who once tried to do something good and ended up doing
something unforgivable.

They say I'm a rescuer.
Zipporah's sisters told their father I saved them.
That I drew water.
That I fought off the shepherds.

Round 3: Moses — The Fight for Calling

Funny how they called me Egyptian.
I didn't even correct them.
What was I supposed to say?

Hi. I'm Moses. Born of slaves. Raised as a prince. Now I run from both.

When my son was born, I named him Gershom.
"I have become a foreigner in a foreign land."

But the truth is, I've always felt foreign.
Even in Egypt.
Even in the palace.
Even in my own skin.

There's a fire in me that won't go out… but I don't know what to do with it.
I tried once.
And it burned everything down.

So now I wait.
I watch the sheep.
I water the flock.

And I wonder…

Was I wrong to care?

Or was I just too early?

The Corner Man Speaks

You looked this way and that.
But you never looked up.

Round 3: Moses — The Fight for Calling

You thought no one saw you.
But I did.

You buried the body in the sand—
but not your heart.
Not your ache.
Not your fire.

You were trying to fight with bare hands what I would one day
command with stretched arms.
You were trying to deliver a people I hadn't yet released.
But I saw you.

Not the polished version.
The real you.

The firestarter.
The misfit.
The man who couldn't ignore injustice, even when it cost him
everything.

You think you failed.
You think you're disqualified.

But listen—what feels like exile is not the end of your story.
It's the beginning of Mine.

Midian is not a punishment.
It's a womb.
It's where I make prophets out of fugitives
and shepherds out of sons.

Round 3: Moses — The Fight for Calling

The cry of My people is rising.
And I'm listening.

But I'm not just preparing *them* for deliverance.
I'm preparing *you* for obedience.

You want to fight?
Then learn how to wait.
You want to lead?
Then learn how to follow.

You are not forgotten, Moses.
You are being formed.

Sit by the well.
Name your ache.
Tend the sheep.

The fire is not out.

It's just not time to speak yet.

But soon…
I will call your name.

Exodus 3:1-22 The Bush That Burned and Spoke

📖 *Exodus 3:1–22*

- God appears to Moses in the burning bush
- Moses is told to return to Egypt
- God reveals His name: *Ehyeh-Asher-Ehyeh* (I Am Who I Am)

Exodus 3:1–22 (NIV)

Now Moses was tending the flock of Jethro his father-in-law, the priest of Midian, and he led the flock to the far side of the wilderness and came to Horeb, the mountain of God. There the angel of the Lord appeared to him in flames of fire from within a bush. Moses saw that though the bush was on fire it did not burn up.

So Moses thought, "I will go over and see this strange sight—why the bush does not burn up."

When the Lord saw that he had gone over to look, God called to him from within the bush, "Moses! Moses!"

And Moses said, "Here I am."

"Do not come any closer," God said. "Take off your sandals, for the place where you are standing is holy ground." Then he said, "I am the God of your father, the God of Abraham, the God of Isaac and the God of Jacob."

At this, Moses hid his face, because he was afraid to look at God.

The Lord said, "I have indeed seen the misery of my people in Egypt. I have heard them crying out because of their slave drivers, and I am concerned about their suffering. So I have come down to rescue them from the hand of the Egyptians and to bring them up out of that land into a good and spacious land, a land flowing with milk and honey—the home of the Canaanites, Hittites, Amorites, Perizzites, Hivites and Jebusites.

And now the cry of the Israelites has reached me, and I have seen the way the Egyptians are oppressing them. So now, go. I am sending you to Pharaoh to bring my people the Israelites out of Egypt."

But Moses said to God, "Who am I that I should go to Pharaoh and bring the Israelites out of Egypt?"

And God said, "I will be with you. And this will be the sign to you that it is I who have sent you: When you have brought the people out of Egypt, you will worship God on this mountain."

Moses said to God, "Suppose I go to the Israelites and say to them, 'The God of your fathers has sent me to you,' and they ask me, 'What is his name?' Then what shall I tell them?"

God said to Moses, "I am who I am. This is what you are to say to the Israelites: 'I am has sent me to you.'"

God also said to Moses, "Say to the Israelites, 'The Lord, the God of your fathers—the God of Abraham, the God of Isaac and the God of Jacob—has sent me to you.'

"This is my name forever, the name you shall call me from generation to generation.

"Go, assemble the elders of Israel and say to them, 'The Lord, the God of your fathers—the God of Abraham, Isaac and Jacob—appeared to me and said: I have watched over you and have seen what has been done to you in Egypt. And I have promised to bring you up out of your misery in Egypt into the land of the Canaanites…a land flowing with milk and honey.'

"The elders of Israel will listen to you. Then you and the elders are to go to the king of Egypt and say to him, 'The Lord, the God of the Hebrews, has met with us. Let us take a three-day journey into the wilderness to offer sacrifices to the Lord our God.'

"But I know that the king of Egypt will not let you go unless a mighty hand compels him. So I will stretch out my hand and strike the Egyptians with all the wonders that I will perform among them. After that, he will let you go.

"And I will make the Egyptians favorably disposed toward this people, so that when you leave you will not go empty-handed. Every woman is to ask her neighbor and any woman living in her house for articles of silver and gold and for clothing, which you will put on your sons and daughters. And so you will plunder the Egyptians."

The Preacher Speaks

Sometimes God doesn't call you in the sanctuary.
Sometimes He finds you on the far side of the wilderness.

That's where Moses was.
Tending sheep that weren't his.
Living in a land that wasn't home.
Two lifetimes behind him—one in Pharaoh's court, one in the shadows—and not much to show for either.
If you'd asked him that morning what his purpose was, he might've said, *"To keep the flock alive and my past buried."*

But that's the thing about calling.
It doesn't ask your permission.
It meets you where you are… and sets something on fire.

Round 3: Moses — The Fight for Calling

Scripture says Moses led the sheep to Horeb, the mountain of God.
But it wasn't a pilgrimage.
He didn't know where he was going.
He was just doing his job.
One foot in front of the other.
The day probably felt like every other day—until it didn't.

There, in the brush, a flame caught his eye.
A bush on fire, but not burning up.

He could've walked on.
He could've chalked it up to the heat or the haze.
But instead, he turned aside.
And when he did, the voice called his name.

"Moses. Moses."

That's when he said it—three words that open every real encounter with God:

"Here I am."

It's easy to forget how human that moment was.

Moses was not standing on a church platform.
He was standing on dirt.
Dusty sandals. Sleeves rolled up.
Still smelling like sheep.

And yet God says:

"Take off your sandals. You're on holy ground."

There was no tabernacle yet. No altar.
Just presence.

Round 3: Moses — The Fight for Calling

And that's always been what makes ground holy.

Not the architecture.
Not the ritual.
But the **presence of the living God**—right there, speaking out of fire to a man who thought his time had passed.

Then came the words Moses hadn't heard in decades:

"I have seen… I have heard… I have come down."

Don't miss that.

This is a God who sees suffering.
Who hears groaning.
Who comes down—not in fury, but in faithfulness.
Not with a sword, but with a name.

God reminds Moses who He is: the God of Abraham, Isaac, and Jacob.
Not a stranger.
Not a new deity.
But the One who remembers covenant.

And then comes the shock.

"I am sending you."

That's when the excuses start.

"Who am I?"

You can hear the scar tissue in the question.

Round 3: Moses — The Fight for Calling

He doesn't ask, *"What should I say?"* or *"Where should I go?"*
He asks, *"Who am I?"*

It's the voice of someone who tried once… and got burned.

But God doesn't flinch.

He doesn't tell Moses what he's capable of.
He tells Moses who will go with him.

"I will be with you."

Because calling is never about our capacity.
It's about God's presence.

Still, Moses presses:

"What if they ask Your name?"

It's not a small question.
In Egypt, every god had a name—and that name told you what the god could do.

But this God answers differently.

"Ehyeh-Asher-Ehyeh."
"I Am Who I Am."

It's a name that isn't tied to place or power or form.
It just… *is.*
Unburning fire.
Unending presence.

Not a god to be managed.
A God to be followed.

So Moses stands there, barefoot and trembling.
The bush still burns.
The sheep still wander nearby.
And the world is about to change.

But right now—this is holy ground.

Not because Moses is ready.
But because God has come near.

The Rabbi Speaks

Come with me.
Not to a temple. Not to Sinai.
To a thicket of dry brush on the far edge of nowhere.

This is where the fire waited.

Not in the palace.
Not in the crowd.
But in the silence after obscurity had done its slow work.

And if Moses hadn't turned,
if he had kept walking,
we would not be having this conversation.

The Hebrew says:

כִּי סָר לִרְאוֹת (*ki sar lirot*)
"When God saw that he turned aside to see…"

Did you catch that?

Round 3: Moses — The Fight for Calling

God didn't speak until Moses turned.
The flame was already burning—but the voice was still silent.
And in this, you learn something the West often forgets:

In the East, revelation waits for response.

It is not delivered.
It is invited.
It does not overpower the senses.
It waits to see who notices.

The word *"sar"* (turned aside) doesn't just mean "glanced."
It implies a deviation from the expected path.
A reorientation. A willingness to stop.

Moses could have shrugged it off as desert heat.
He could have thought, *"Strange, but not my concern."*

Instead, he steps toward the flame.

And only then—*only then*—does the voice call his name:

"Moses. Moses."

Now we must talk about names.

When Moses asks, *"Who shall I say sent me?"*
he's not asking for God's business card.
He's asking, *"What kind of God are You?"*
Because in Egypt, names carry domains. Power. Boundaries.

But God gives him something else:

Round 3: Moses — The Fight for Calling

אֶהְיֶה אֲשֶׁר אֶהְיֶה (*Ehyeh-Asher-Ehyeh*)
"I Am Who I Am."

Or more literally:
"I will be what I will be."

This is not static identity.
This is *becoming*.
This is future-infused, mystery-laced, ever-burning Being.

Not a god of wood or stone.
Not a formula.
A presence.
A fire that speaks but does not consume.

Now step closer. Take off your sandals.
Why?

Because in Hebrew, the word for "sandals" (*na'al*) shares a root with "locked" or "closed off."

To remove your sandals is not just a hygiene ritual.
It is a symbolic gesture:
Open yourself. Uncover what you've covered. Step as you are.

And where does this happen?

"For the place where you are standing is holy ground."

There is no temple here.
No altar.
No liturgy.

The only thing that makes it holy is that **God is here—**
and someone bothered to notice.

Western minds often ask, *"Is this the moment Moses is called?"*
But in Hebraic thought, calling is not a point—it is a process.
The bush burns because the fire began long ago.
This is not the start.
It is the *unveiling.*

And what of the mission?

"I have seen... I have heard... I have come down... I am sending you."

God is not a passive deity.
He is moved.
He is active.
But He chooses to move **through** the ones who are willing to turn aside.

So then, student—ask yourself this:

How many bushes have burned beside your path?
How many flames have danced just beyond your peripheral vision?
And what might heaven still be waiting to say—
if only you would turn?

The Fighter Speaks

I didn't go looking for a burning bush.

I was just doing what I always do—
wake up, tend sheep, keep moving.
It's a quiet life, far from the man I used to be.
And most days, that's a relief.

Round 3: Moses — The Fight for Calling

But then… the flame.
Not a flash. Not an explosion.
Just something out of the corner of my eye.
A flicker that wouldn't go out.

At first, I thought I imagined it.
I almost kept walking.
But something in me… turned.

I didn't expect a voice.

Especially not that voice.
The kind that doesn't just echo in your ears,
but folds itself into your bones.

"Moses. Moses."

I hadn't heard my name like that in years.
Not in anger.
Not in accusation.
But in… recognition.

It undid me.

Then came the words that stopped me cold:

"Take off your sandals… this is holy ground."

I hadn't thought of myself as holy in a long time.
Not since Egypt.
Not since the body in the sand.
Not since my people turned their backs on me and I ran.

Round 3: Moses — The Fight for Calling

But now—this desert dirt is holy?
This broken man is being called by the God of Abraham?

I couldn't breathe.
I couldn't speak.
I covered my face like a child caught looking at something too bright.

Because that's what it felt like—
like light was breaking through the cracks I'd spent forty years sealing
shut.

Then He said the thing I didn't know I still needed to hear:

"I have seen their misery… I have heard their cry… I have come down."

I thought He had forgotten.
I thought I had failed.
I thought it was too late.

But now He's saying I'm part of the plan?

That I'm supposed to *go back*?

Back to Egypt?
Back to Pharaoh?
Back to the people who didn't want me?

I said it before I could stop myself:

"Who am I?"

Because I honestly didn't know anymore.
I'm not a prince.

I'm not a leader.
I'm not a prophet.

I'm a man who ran.
A man with more past than future.
A man who's been talking to sheep for forty years, and suddenly hears fire speak.

He didn't argue.

He just said:

"I will be with you."

And somehow, those five words felt heavier than the weight of the call.

He would go with me.
But He wouldn't go instead of me.

This wasn't a rescue.
It was an invitation.
To walk back into the place of my greatest fear…
because His name would go before me.

I still don't know if I'm ready.
But I know I've been called.

And I know the bush burned…
and did not burn out.

Just like something inside me.

The Corner Man Speaks

Round 3: Moses — The Fight for Calling

I never stopped watching you, Moses.

Not when you buried the Egyptian.
Not when you ran.
Not when your voice grew quiet in Midian and you started calling
yourself a foreigner.

You thought your story was over.
But I was just waiting—
for the moment you'd turn aside.

You didn't need a map.
You didn't need a priest.
You just needed to notice the fire.

Because I don't shout over the noise.
I burn beside the path.

And when you looked... really looked...
I knew you were ready.

You took off your sandals because I asked.
But I was already there—
in the dust,
in the wilderness,
in the years you thought I'd forgotten.

I saw every tear the Hebrews shed.
I heard every groan in Egypt.
And I heard every question you asked in exile.

Round 3: Moses — The Fight for Calling

"Why me?"
"Why now?"
"Why this ache that never leaves?"

Now you know.

Because what burned in you as a boy—
I've kept alive.

What felt like disqualification—
I've turned into preparation.

You want to know My name?

I will be who I will be.
Not just in power, but in presence.
Not just for Israel, but for you.

I will be with you—
when you speak to Pharaoh,
when you tremble in doubt,
when the people grumble and the path narrows and the fire burns
again.

You don't have to carry the plan.
Just My name.

You don't have to change the world.
Just say yes when I speak.

You turned aside once, Moses.
Keep turning.

Round 3: Moses — The Fight for Calling

And I will meet you there—
again
and again
and again.

Exodus 4:1-17 Lips of Clay, Hands of Fire

📖 *Exodus 4:1–17*

- Moses protests: "I can't speak."
- God gives signs: staff into serpent, leprous hand healed
- Aaron is appointed as mouthpiece—but the call remains Moses'
- Resistance is met with divine anger—and grace

Exodus 4:1–17 (NIV)

Moses answered, "What if they do not believe me or listen to me and say, 'The Lord did not appear to you'?"

Then the Lord said to him, "What is that in your hand?"

"A staff," he replied.

The Lord said, "Throw it on the ground."

Moses threw it on the ground and it became a snake, and he ran from it.

Then the Lord said to him, "Reach out your hand and take it by the tail." So Moses reached out and took hold of the snake and it turned back into a staff in his hand.

"This," said the Lord, "is so that they may believe that the Lord, the God of their fathers—the God of Abraham, the God of Isaac and the God of Jacob—has appeared to you."

Then the Lord said, "Put your hand inside your cloak." So Moses put his hand into his cloak, and when he took it out, the skin was leprous—it had become as white as snow.

"Now put it back into your cloak," he said. So Moses put his hand back into his cloak, and when he took it out, it was restored, like the rest of his flesh.

Then the Lord said, "If they do not believe you or pay attention to the first sign, they may believe the second. But if they do not believe these two signs or listen to you, take some water from the Nile and pour it on the dry ground. The water you take from the river will become blood on the ground."

Moses said to the Lord, "Pardon your servant, Lord. I have never been eloquent, neither in the past nor since you have spoken to your servant. I am slow of speech and tongue."

The Lord said to him, "Who gave human beings their mouths? Who makes them deaf or mute? Who gives them sight or makes them blind? Is it not I, the Lord? Now go; I will help you speak and will teach you what to say."

But Moses said, "Pardon your servant, Lord. Please send someone else."

Then the Lord's anger burned against Moses and he said, "What about your brother, Aaron the Levite? I know he can speak well. He is already on his way to meet you, and he will be glad to see you. You shall speak to him and put words in his mouth; I will help both of you speak and will teach you what to do. He will speak to the people for you, and it will be as if he were your mouth and as if you were God to him. But take this staff in your hand so you can perform the signs with it."

The Preacher Speaks

There's something tender—almost heartbreaking—about this scene.

God has just spoken His name.
He's revealed His presence.

Round 3: Moses — The Fight for Calling

He's declared His intention to rescue His people.
And now, with all of heaven leaning in… Moses hesitates.

He doesn't say no.
But he doesn't say yes either.
He says, *"What if they don't believe me?"*

And suddenly we're not standing on holy ground anymore.
We're standing on the battlefield of insecurity.

It's easy to forget that most of God's greatest moves begin not with confidence,
but with trembling.

Moses isn't stubborn here. He's scared.
Not of Pharaoh.
Of failure.

He's been dismissed before.
He's been misunderstood.
And when you've spent decades second-guessing your own voice,
you don't suddenly find it just because fire spoke.

So God does something beautiful.

He doesn't argue with Moses' fear.
He just draws his attention to what's already in his hand.

"What is that in your hand?"

Moses says, "A staff."
Simple. Familiar. Ordinary.
The tool of a shepherd. The symbol of a fugitive's quiet life.

God says, *"Throw it down."*

When he does, it turns into a snake—and Moses runs.
Because that's what happens when you finally see the power that was dormant in your own grip.

But God doesn't let him run for long.

"Pick it up by the tail."

It's not just a trick.
It's a training.

God is showing Moses:
What I ask of you may feel dangerous, but you are not alone.
What you release in obedience, I will return to you in power.

Then comes the second sign—his hand made leprous and then healed.
Not just a display for others, but a mirror for Moses.

This isn't about magic.
It's about trust.
God is revealing: *"I can transform what's broken. Even what's closest to you. Even what you hide."*

And still, Moses isn't ready.

He says:

"Pardon your servant, Lord. I've never been eloquent."

There it is.
The old wound.
The disqualifier he carries like a scar on his tongue.

Round 3: Moses — The Fight for Calling

He's afraid he won't be enough.
That he won't speak clearly.
That he won't be believed.
That he'll be sent back into the place of his greatest failure—without the voice to carry the call.

And God responds, not with rebuke, but with a question:

"Who gave human beings their mouths?"

This isn't a dismissal.
It's a reminder: *"I know how I made you."*

Then God says:

"Now go; I will help you speak and will teach you what to say."

But Moses still can't do it.

"Please send someone else."

And here, for the first time, God's anger burns.

Not because Moses is weak.
But because Moses won't believe what God is offering him.

And yet even then—
God does not walk away.

He brings in Aaron.
A brother. A mouthpiece. A partner.
Grace, even in resistance.

But He doesn't release Moses from the call.

"Take this staff in your hand…"

Still the staff.
Still the sign.
Still the call.

Because God knows that obedience doesn't always start with boldness. Sometimes it starts with fear... and the courage to keep holding the thing He told you not to let go of.

The Rabbi Speaks

You Western students like your heroes certain.
You want your prophets with straight backs and steady hands.
But come sit here, in the sand.
Let me show you a man called by fire... still dragging the ashes of his failure behind him.

This is not the Moses of Charlton Heston.
This is not the lawgiver on Sinai.
This is a stammering exile—arguing with the voice that burns without burning him.

And here is the first great paradox of calling:

He is chosen... but he resists.

Moses opens his mouth not with praise, but protest.

"What if they don't believe me?"

Now you must understand something:
In Egyptian court, a man without credentials is nothing.
Truth is validated by power.
Presence is authenticated by performance.

Round 3: Moses — The Fight for Calling

So when Moses asks this question, he's not being petty.
He is carrying the trauma of rejection—not just by Pharaoh, but by his own people.

And what does God do?

He doesn't scold.
He doesn't shout.
He simply says:

"What is that in your hand?"

Now pay attention.

The Hebrew here is:

מַה־זֶּה בְיָדֶךָ (*mah-zeh v'yadekha*)
"What is this in your hand?"

Not *What do you wish you had?*
Not *What would you use if you were ready?*
But *What do you already carry?*

This is how the God of Israel works.
He takes what you've been using for survival… and turns it into a sign.

Moses throws the staff to the ground.
It becomes a serpent.
He runs.

Yes—Moses runs from the very thing he's just been holding.

This is not just fear.
This is the Hebraic pattern of revelation:

Round 3: Moses — The Fight for Calling

What you think you control... is not tame.
What you grip for safety... might bite when exposed.

But God tells him:

"Pick it up by the tail."

No shepherd would do this.
The tail is the most dangerous place to grab a snake.

But this is not about technique.
This is about **trust**.

The second sign?
His hand becomes leprous—*white as snow*—then is healed.

In Hebrew, the word for leprosy here is צָרַעַת (*tzara'at*).
It doesn't always refer to disease as you understand it today.
It often represents something deeper: **exposure**.
An unveiling of what's hidden beneath the surface.

God is saying:

"I can reveal what is broken.
I can restore what is hidden.
I can use even your hand—the hand that once killed—to heal."

But still... Moses says no.

"I'm slow of speech. I can't talk."

Now remember—Moses was raised in Pharaoh's court.
He likely knew multiple languages.

Round 3: Moses — The Fight for Calling

This is not about grammar.
This is about shame.

In the East, we say a man's tongue reveals his heart.
Moses isn't afraid of public speaking.
He's afraid of not being believed.

And yet, God does not change His mind.
He reminds Moses:

"Who gave man his mouth?"

The Hebrew here is poetic, pointed:

מִי שָׂם פֶּה לָאָדָם (*Mi sam peh l'adam?*)
"Who placed a mouth in man?"

God is not asking for permission.
He is declaring authorship.

Even after all this, Moses pleads:

"Please send someone else."

And God's anger burns.

But do you notice what He does?

He does not strike Moses down.
He gives him Aaron.

This is the final paradox in the passage:

God's anger is real—but so is His mercy.
He does not cancel Moses. He completes him.
Through partnership. Through grace.

Now take this last piece with you:

"Take the staff in your hand..."

The staff hasn't changed.
But now Moses knows what it can do.

Because now, it's not just a stick.
It's a story.

Of fear.
Of fire.
Of a God who calls through weakness—
and answers with presence.

The Fighter Speaks

I didn't want the fire anymore.

Not after Egypt.
Not after the mistake.
Not after the silence.

I'd spent half a lifetime learning how to live without being called.
And now the Voice won't stop speaking.

"What if they don't believe me?"

It wasn't a question.
It was a scar.

I remember what it felt like the first time—
when I tried to stand up for my people...
and they turned on me.

Round 3: Moses — The Fight for Calling

"Who made you ruler and judge over us?"

That wound still stings.
I buried it beneath years of shepherding, of hiding.
But it never left.

So when I said those words,
I wasn't doubting God.
I was doubting me.

He asked me what was in my hand.

Just a staff.
That's all it's ever been.

A shepherd's rod.
A walking stick.
A piece of wood that helped me stay upright in rocky places.

And when He told me to throw it down, I did.

I didn't expect it to change.
I didn't expect it to strike back.

But it turned into a snake—
and something in me panicked.

Not because it was dangerous,
but because it reminded me I wasn't in control.

Then He said the craziest thing:

"Pick it up… by the tail."

Round 3: Moses — The Fight for Calling

Even a boy in Egypt knows better than that.
You don't grab power from behind.

But something in His tone made me obey.
I reached out, trembling…
and it became what it always was—
but now, different.

Holy.
Alive.
Charged with something I didn't understand.

Then my hand.

One second it was flesh.
The next, ruined.
Leprous. Isolated. Untouchable.

And then—restored.

Like nothing had ever happened…
and yet everything had.

I stared at my palm for a long time.

Because that's the part of me I used to kill a man.
That's the part of me I've hidden for forty years.
And He just healed it like it was always meant to be used for something
better.

I should've trusted Him after that.
But I couldn't.

Round 3: Moses — The Fight for Calling

"I don't speak well," I told Him.
"I never have."

Because the truth is, I've never liked my own voice.

Too slow.
Too unsure.
Too heavy with regret.

But He just asked me who made mouths in the first place.

"I will be with you," He said.
"I will help you speak."

Still… I begged.

"Please send someone else."

And that's when His voice changed.

Not rage.
But fire, pressed in tight.

"What about Aaron?"

I didn't know Aaron was coming.
I hadn't seen him in years.

But God did.

He knew I would need help.
He knew I'd falter.
He knew I'd still go.

Because I wasn't ready.
But I was chosen.

I still don't feel worthy.
But I'm holding the staff.

I'm still scared.
But the hand that once trembled is now steady.

And when I speak—
whether through my brother's mouth or my own—
He will be there.

That's the only thing I'm sure of anymore.
And maybe... that's enough.

The Corner Man Speaks

You thought the fire was the hard part.

But it's not the fire that breaks a man.
It's the calling.

You're not afraid of Pharaoh, Moses.
You're afraid of being seen—really seen.
Afraid that the weight of your past will crack the voice I'm trying to
give you.

But I didn't ask you to be eloquent.
I asked you to trust Me.

That fear you carry—
the one you think disqualifies you?
I'm not trying to erase it.
I'm trying to *redeem* it.

Round 3: Moses — The Fight for Calling

That staff you've leaned on?
Throw it down.
Let it become what it really is.
Not just a shepherd's tool…
but a sign that power grows from obedience, not confidence.

That hand you hide?
Let Me touch it.
Let Me show you what I can heal, even in the parts you're ashamed to reveal.

I know you're tired.
I know the weight feels too much.
But I'm not walking away just because you pushed back.

I am not the kind of God who calls once and then moves on.
I call again.
And again.
And again.

And when your voice cracks—
I send your brother.

When your hands shake—
I place a staff in them.

When your faith is smaller than your fear—
I don't wait for it to grow before I move.

I move anyway.

I'm not looking for perfection.
I'm looking for surrender.

Round 3: Moses — The Fight for Calling

I don't need you to impress Pharaoh.
I need you to trust Me in front of him.

Take the staff.
Take the fear.
Take the fire.

And walk forward, even if your knees tremble.

You're not going alone.

I will be with you.
Not just in the miracle.
But in the stutter.
In the sweat.
In the step.

This is the ring.
And I am still in your corner.

Exodus 5:1-23 Let My People Go

📖 *Exodus 5:1–23*

- Moses and Aaron confront Pharaoh
- Pharaoh doubles the Israelites' burdens
- The people turn on Moses
- Moses turns back to God, defeated and confused

Exodus 5:1–23 (NIV)

Afterward Moses and Aaron went to Pharaoh and said, "This is what the Lord, the God of Israel, says: 'Let my people go, so that they may hold a festival to me in the wilderness.'"

Pharaoh said, "Who is the Lord, that I should obey him and let Israel go? I do not know the Lord and I will not let Israel go."

Then they said, "The God of the Hebrews has met with us. Now let us take a three-day journey into the wilderness to offer sacrifices to the Lord our God, or he may strike us with plagues or with the sword."

But the king of Egypt said, "Moses and Aaron, why are you taking the people away from their labor? Get back to your work!" Then Pharaoh said, "Look, the people of the land are now numerous, and you are stopping them from working."

That same day Pharaoh gave this order to the slave drivers and overseers in charge of the people: "You are no longer to supply the people with straw for making bricks; let them go and gather their own straw. But require them to make the same number of bricks as before; don't reduce the quota. They are lazy; that is why they are crying out, 'Let us go and sacrifice to our God.' Make the work harder for the people so that they keep working and pay no attention to lies."

Round 3: Moses — The Fight for Calling

Then the slave drivers and the overseers went out and said to the people, "This is what Pharaoh says: I will not give you any more straw. Go and get your own straw wherever you can find it, but your work will not be reduced at all." So the people scattered all over Egypt to gather stubble to use for straw. The slave drivers kept pressing them, saying, "Complete the work required of you for each day, just as when you had straw." And Pharaoh's slave drivers beat the Israelite overseers they had appointed, demanding, "Why haven't you met your quota of bricks yesterday or today, as before?"

Then the Israelite overseers went and appealed to Pharaoh: "Why have you treated your servants this way? Your servants are given no straw, yet we are told, 'Make bricks!' Your servants are being beaten, but the fault is with your own people."

Pharaoh said, "Lazy, that's what you are—lazy! That is why you keep saying, 'Let us go and sacrifice to the Lord.' Now get to work. You will not be given any straw, yet you must produce your full quota of bricks."

The Israelite overseers realized they were in trouble when they were told, "You are not to reduce the number of bricks required of you for each day." When they left Pharaoh, they found Moses and Aaron waiting to meet them, and they said, "May the Lord look on you and judge you! You have made us obnoxious to Pharaoh and his officials and have put a sword in their hand to kill us."

Moses returned to the Lord and said, "Why, Lord, why have you brought trouble on this people? Is this why you sent me? Ever since I went to Pharaoh to speak in your name, he has brought trouble on this people, and you have not rescued your people at all."

The Preacher Speaks

There's a moment in every calling when things get worse before they get better.

This is that moment.

Moses obeys.
He stands before Pharaoh.
He says the words God told him to say:

"Let my people go."

But instead of breakthrough, he gets backlash.
Instead of freedom, more chains.
Instead of a softened heart, Pharaoh doubles the workload and hardens his grip.

You'd think this would be the chapter where obedience is rewarded.
But that's not how it goes.

This chapter isn't about victory.
It's about disappointment.
It's about the moment when obedience costs you… before it changes anything.

And the truth is—most of us weren't taught to expect this.
We were told that if we trust God, things will get better.
That faith makes life smoother, cleaner, safer.

But that's not the pattern of scripture.
That's the promise of marketing.

Round 3: Moses — The Fight for Calling

In real covenant stories, the first step of obedience often leads straight into confrontation.

God told Moses He would be with him.
He didn't say Pharaoh would listen.
He didn't say the people would cheer.

And that's exactly what happens.

Moses steps into the palace and speaks.
Pharaoh mocks:

"Who is the Lord, that I should obey him?"

He's not just rejecting Moses.
He's rejecting God's authority altogether.

This is the first real fight of the Exodus story.
It's not physical.
It's theological.

Then Pharaoh does something cruel. Calculated.

He tells the slave drivers to remove the straw from the brickmaking process.

"Make them gather their own."

The quota stays the same.
The labor doubles.
The burden breaks.

This is what oppression always does.
It increases pressure, then blames the victim for not keeping up.

Round 3: Moses — The Fight for Calling

And the people—Moses' own people—turn on him.

They say:

"You've made us stink in Pharaoh's sight. You've handed him the sword to kill us."

That line cuts.

Moses came with a word from the Lord…
and now he's being blamed for making everything worse.

This is the lonely part of leadership.
The part no one prepares you for.

When you say yes to God, and your yes doesn't work like you hoped it would.

So Moses does what most of us would do.

He turns to God—not in praise, but in protest.

"Why have You brought trouble on this people? Is this why You sent me?"

He's not trying to be dramatic.
He's trying to understand.

Because from his vantage point, nothing is working.

He obeyed.
He spoke.
And now the people are suffering more than before.

"You have not rescued Your people at all."

It's an honest prayer.
A wounded one.

And God doesn't silence him.
God lets him bring it.

Because lament is not rebellion—it's relationship refusing to let go.

This chapter reminds us:

- Obedience is not always rewarded quickly.

- Backlash does not mean failure.

- And sometimes, the darkest moment in the story… comes right before God says, "Now, watch what I do."

The Rabbi Speaks

Come.

Sit with me for a moment—not on the palace steps, but at the edge of the slave yard.
Feel the dust.
Hear the whip.
Smell the sweat of a people who've forgotten how to hope.

This is not the story most of your Western teachers emphasize.

You were told that obedience unlocks favor.
That when God speaks, doors open.
But in the East, we read slower.

We see the pattern.

First the call. Then the resistance.
First the Word. Then the weight.

Round 3: Moses — The Fight for Calling

When Moses and Aaron approach Pharaoh, they speak not as rebels, but as messengers:

כֹּה אָמַר יְהוָה אֱלֹהֵי יִשְׂרָאֵל
"Thus says YHWH, the God of Israel…"

But Pharaoh's response slices like a blade:

מִי יְהוָה, אֲשֶׁר אֶשְׁמַע בְּקֹלוֹ?
"Who is YHWH, that I should listen to His voice?"
"I do not know YHWH, and I will not let Israel go."

This is not just defiance.
This is cosmic arrogance.

Pharaoh is not confused. He is making a claim:

"I am the god here. My voice rules this land. Yours is foreign, invisible, weak."

And what does Moses do?

He holds the line.
He repeats the message.

But Pharaoh answers with a counterpunch—not with philosophy, but with force.

"Make the work harder."

He doesn't challenge Moses' theology.
He challenges the people's capacity to believe.

Because if you crush a people's breath,
they won't waste it on worship.

Now listen carefully.

There's a Hebrew word repeated through this passage:

תַּפְרִיעוּ (tafri'u) — "to disrupt, to loosen, to distract."

Pharaoh says Moses is *distracting* the people.
Pulling them away from productivity.
Filling their heads with lies about festivals and freedom.

Sound familiar?

Even today, systems of empire will label prophets as troublemakers—
will call worship "waste,"
will say rest is laziness,
will treat trust in God as sedition.

Pharaoh hasn't disappeared.
He's just changed clothes.

And when the people are crushed…
they turn on Moses.

Can you blame them?

Slaves don't know how to receive a rescue they didn't ask for.
When you've been surviving in oppression long enough,
deliverance can feel like disruption.

So Moses prays.

Round 3: Moses — The Fight for Calling

But listen—this is not a Western "prayer."
This is a Hebraic *lament*.

"Why have You brought this evil on the people? Why did You even send me?"

In Hebrew:

לָמָה הֲרֵעֹתָה לָעָם הַזֶּה
"Why have You done evil to this people?"

Moses uses strong language.
Accusatory language.
But do not mistake it for faithlessness.

This is what we call חֻצְפָּה (*chutzpah*)—holy boldness.
The courage to speak to God as if He's still in the conversation.
Because He is.

Western theology often avoids this level of honesty.
But in our tradition, protest is not rejection—it's *participation*.

We do not shout because we've stopped believing.
We shout because we know Who's listening.

Remember this:

Obedience often brings you into the fight, not out of it.
And lament is not weakness. It is covenant… spoken with bruised lips.

The Fighter Speaks

I said what You told me to say.

Round 3: Moses — The Fight for Calling

I stood there, chest tight, palms sweating, heart pounding—
and I said it.
I spoke Your name in front of Pharaoh.

"Let my people go."

And I waited.
For something.
Anything.

A pause.
A tremble.
A crack in his stone heart.

But there was nothing.

He didn't even blink.

He mocked You.

"Who is the Lord?"

He laughed in Your face—
and I stood there, humiliated, holding Your words like a broken staff.

I thought I was doing the right thing.
I thought saying yes would matter.
I thought obedience would change something.

Instead... it made everything worse.

Now they're working harder.
No straw. Same quota.
Beaten. Bruised. Blamed.

Round 3: Moses — The Fight for Calling

And when the people saw me waiting outside Pharaoh's court…
their faces—
they weren't angry.

They were betrayed.

They didn't need to speak.
Their eyes said it:

"You did this."

And they're not wrong.

God, I didn't ask for this.

I was content in Midian.
Sheep don't argue.
Fire stays in the sky.

But You lit that bush.
You called me back.

And I… I believed You.

I believed You were going to rescue them.
I believed I might finally matter again.

But now?

Now the people suffer more.
And I'm the face they blame.

So I asked You:

Round 3: Moses — The Fight for Calling

"Why have You brought this trouble?"
"Is this why You sent me?"

I wasn't trying to dishonor You.
I just needed to know—
is this how You work?

Do You stir up faith just to let it get crushed?

Do You call the broken just to have them break again?

Because it feels like I stepped into a fight I was never strong enough
for.
And now the blood's on my hands.

I still want to believe You.
I do.
But right now, I don't know how.

I thought Your name would shake the gates.

Instead, it cracked my confidence.

And if You're still here—if You're still listening—
then I need more than a command.

I need presence.
I need power.
I need a reason to go back in that ring.

Because right now, it feels like I lost the first round...
and I don't know if I have another one in me.

The Corner Man Speaks

Round 3: Moses — The Fight for Calling

You did what I asked.
And it didn't go the way you thought it would.

I know.
I saw Pharaoh's face.
I heard his mockery.
I felt the weight of every brick he laid on their backs.

And I stayed.

I didn't leave the room when your words fell flat.
I didn't flinch when the crowd turned.
I stayed right beside you—because this fight was never yours alone.

You spoke My name, Moses.

You stepped back into the palace that once held your shame,
and you spoke words that carried eternity in them.

Don't confuse silence for absence.
Don't confuse backlash for failure.

Pharaoh didn't ignore you because I'm weak.
He resisted you because I'm real.

The darkness always tightens its grip when the light starts to move.

You think obedience should make life easier.
But this isn't a formula.
It's a war.

And in war, the first move doesn't win the battle.
It draws the lines.

Round 3: Moses — The Fight for Calling

It reveals the resistance.
It exposes the heart of the oppressor… and the pain of the oppressed.

You needed to see this.
So did they.

Because I'm not just freeing bodies.
I'm breaking lies.

Yes, they're angry with you.
Yes, they're afraid.
But I can handle that.

I'm not just their Deliverer.
I'm their Healer.
And healing always begins with honesty.

They cried out to Me once before.
Now they'll cry again.

And this time—
they'll know Who's listening.

Moses, you're asking Me why I sent you.

Here's why:

Because I knew you wouldn't run when it got hard.
I knew you'd bring your ache back to Me.
I knew you'd stay in the ring—bruised, yes, but still looking for My face.

Round 3: Moses — The Fight for Calling

You're not failing.
You're fighting.
And this fight isn't over.

Now take a breath.
Wipe the dust off your sandals.

We've only just begun.

The name you carry still burns.
And I'm still in your corner.

Exodus 6:1-13 The Name That Wrestles

📖 *Exodus 6:1–13*

- God reaffirms His name and covenant
- "I am the Lord, and I will bring you out…"
- Moses still doubts. The people still don't listen.
- But the fight shifts. Now, Moses begins to speak—not for himself, but for the Name.

Exodus 6:1–13 (NIV)

Then the Lord said to Moses, "Now you will see what I will do to Pharaoh: Because of my mighty hand he will let them go; because of my mighty hand he will drive them out of his country."

God also said to Moses, "I am the Lord. I appeared to Abraham, to Isaac and to Jacob as God Almighty, but by my name the Lord I did not make myself fully known to them. I also established my covenant with them to give them the land of Canaan, where they resided as foreigners. Moreover, I have heard the groaning of the Israelites, whom the Egyptians are enslaving, and I have remembered my covenant.

"Therefore, say to the Israelites: 'I am the Lord, and I will bring you out from under the yoke of the Egyptians. I will free you from being slaves to them, and I will redeem you with an outstretched arm and with mighty acts of judgment. I will take you as my own people, and I will be your God. Then you will know that I am the Lord your God, who brought you out from under the yoke of the Egyptians. And I will bring you to the land I swore with uplifted hand to give to Abraham, to Isaac and to Jacob. I will give it to you as a possession. I am the Lord.'"

Moses reported this to the Israelites, but they did not listen to him because of their discouragement and harsh labor.

Then the Lord said to Moses, "Go, tell Pharaoh king of Egypt to let the Israelites go out of his country."

But Moses said to the Lord, "If the Israelites will not listen to me, why would Pharaoh listen to me, since I speak with faltering lips?"

Now the Lord spoke to Moses and Aaron about the Israelites and Pharaoh king of Egypt, and he commanded them to bring the Israelites out of Egypt.

The Preacher Speaks

Exodus 6:1–13 – The Name That Wrestles *(Rewritten Slow and Steady)*

Let's walk this one carefully.

Moses has done what God asked.
He returned to Egypt.
He spoke to Pharaoh.
He carried the word of the Lord with trembling hands and a borrowed tongue.

And nothing went the way he expected.

Pharaoh's heart grew harder.
The people's burdens grew heavier.
And Moses' confidence began to collapse.

So he does what many of us do when our obedience seems to make things worse—
he turns back to God, confused, frustrated, afraid.

"Why have You brought this trouble?"
"Is this why You sent me?"

Round 3: Moses — The Fight for Calling

God does not scold him.
He doesn't send Moses away to get his attitude in order.
He doesn't ignore the cry.

Instead, He speaks.

And what He says… isn't new.

It's ancient.

God reintroduces Himself.

"I am the Lord."

That's not just a name.
That's a covenant marker.
It's the name He gave at the bush—*YHWH*—the One who is, who was, and who will be.

God is saying:
Moses, I haven't changed. And neither has My promise.

Then He anchors Moses in the story that came before.

"I appeared to Abraham… to Isaac… to Jacob…"
"I established My covenant with them…"

He's reminding Moses that this isn't an isolated event.
This is the continuation of a long, unfolding promise.
The covenant wasn't just for them. It's for now.

"I have heard their groaning…"
"I have remembered…"

Round 3: Moses — The Fight for Calling

Not remembered as in *"I forgot."*
But remembered as in *"I'm moving now."*

The time for fulfillment has come.

Now watch this closely.
God gives Moses a string of declarations.
Seven of them.

Each begins the same way:

"I will…"

Listen:

"I will bring you out."
"I will free you."
"I will redeem you."
"I will take you as My people."
"I will be your God."
"I will bring you to the land."
"I will give it to you."

This isn't motivational speech.
This is covenant language—deliberate, structured, and rooted in God's own name.

God is binding Himself to these promises.
Not based on Moses' performance.
Not based on Israel's response.
But based on His unshakable faithfulness.

And Moses delivers the message.

Round 3: Moses — The Fight for Calling

He says everything God told him to say.

But the people…
they don't listen.

And the text tells us why.

"…because of their discouragement and harsh labor."

In Hebrew: קֹצֶר רוּחַ (*qotzer ruach*) — literally, *"shortness of spirit"* or *"shortness of breath."*

They were crushed.

Not just physically.
Spiritually.

They couldn't catch their breath long enough to believe again.

This is one of the great tragedies of trauma:
Even hope can feel threatening when you've been hurt long enough.

And Moses—he feels the rejection in his bones.

He tells God:

"If they won't listen to me, why would Pharaoh?"
"I'm still not the right man. My lips still falter."

In other words:

"I'm not strong enough to carry this. I told You that at the bush."

But God doesn't debate him.
He doesn't revisit the excuses.
He doesn't even soften the blow.

He simply says:

"Go. Bring them out."

This is what it means to wrestle with the Name.

To stand between what God has said…
and what hasn't yet changed.

To carry a promise that feels too heavy for your chest.
To speak when no one's listening.
To obey when it doesn't work.

But here's what we hold to:

The name of the Lord is not a theory.
It's a tether.
A truth that holds when everything else breaks.

So we keep walking.
We keep speaking.
We keep trusting the One who said:

"I will."

The Rabbi Speaks

Come closer.

Not everything holy is loud.
Some truths arrive like a whisper,
when the fight has gone quiet
and the breath has gone shallow.

Round 3: Moses — The Fight for Calling

This is not just the story of Moses.
It's the story of anyone who has tried to speak God's words
and watched the world stay the same.

The moment begins with a promise—but also with a pivot.

Moses is disoriented.
The people have turned on him.
Pharaoh has not moved.
And the name of God, once burning on his tongue, now trembles in
the silence.

Then God says:

עַתָּה תִרְאֶה אֲשֶׁר אֶעֱשֶׂה לְפַרְעֹה
"Now you will see what I will do to Pharaoh…"

Now, not after your speech worked.
Not once the people believe again.
Now—when nothing has changed on the surface.

This is a Hebraic rhythm:

Revelation follows obedience—not success.
God doesn't wait for everything to align.
He speaks into the chaos.

But what God says next is not tactical.
It's not a plan.

It's a reintroduction.

"I am YHWH."

Round 3: Moses — The Fight for Calling

He repeats it four times in thirteen verses.

This is not redundancy.
This is covenant reinforcement.

We often translate **YHWH** as "I Am,"
but the name carries layers.

It is past, present, and future.
It is promise wrapped in presence.
It is *He Who Was, Who Is, and Who Will Be.*

He says:

"I appeared to Abraham, Isaac, and Jacob as El Shaddai..."
"...but by My name YHWH, I was not fully known to them."

This doesn't mean they never heard the name.
It means they never saw it fulfilled in this way.

They knew the promise.
Moses will see the performance.

Then God speaks seven *"I will"* statements.

This is covenant language.
Structured. Purposeful. Liturgical.

In Hebrew, this list becomes the foundation of the **Passover seder—**
four of those "I will" statements are still recited at Jewish tables to this
day.

"I will bring you out."
"I will deliver you."
"I will redeem you."
"I will take you as My people..."

Round 3: Moses — The Fight for Calling

These are not casual assurances.
They are vows.
Declarations not just of action—but of identity.

God is not merely rescuing slaves.
He is forming a people.

And the center of that formation...
is *His Name*.

But then we come to a grief-laden verse.

"But they did not listen to Moses because of their discouragement and cruel bondage."

In Hebrew:

מִקֹּצֶר רוּחַ וּמֵעֲבֹדָה קָשָׁה
"Because of shortness of spirit and harsh labor."

קֹצֶר רוּחַ (*qotzer ruach*) doesn't just mean emotional exhaustion.
It means breathlessness.
Like a person who's been held underwater too long.

Their trauma has narrowed their lungs.
Hope cannot find a way in.

You must understand this:

In the East, belief is not measured by mental assent—
but by the ability to hold breath in suffering.

And in this moment, they cannot.
Their ruach—their spirit—is constricted.

Even a divine name feels too heavy to carry.

Moses feels it.

The people won't listen.
Pharaoh won't budge.
And his own voice feels broken again.

He says:

"Behold, I am of uncircumcised lips."

That phrase—**עֲרַל שְׂפָתַיִם**—means more than speech trouble.
It's a statement of shame.
Of spiritual disqualification.
As if he's saying,

"My mouth is still unworthy. Nothing has changed."

But God doesn't entertain it.
He commands:

"Speak again. Tell Pharaoh. Bring them out."

Why?

Because the fight is not over.
Because covenant does not depend on how well you feel,
or how fully others respond.

Because **YHWH** is not a name that folds when the breath is short.

It is the name that wrestles.
The name that endures.
The name that carries bruised people through the dark

until breath returns
and songs rise again.

The Fighter Speaks

He said it again.

"I am the Lord."

Like I was supposed to feel something when He said it.
Like just hearing the name again would steady my hands or silence the
doubt.

But it didn't.

Not this time.

I tried to believe Him.
I really did.

He sounded so sure.
Seven "I will" promises—
one after another, like thunder.

"I will bring you out…"
"I will redeem you…"
"I will take you as My people…"

They were beautiful words.

But when I turned to repeat them—
to speak them to the people I was sent to save—
they looked through me.

Empty eyes.
Shallow breath.

Round 3: Moses — The Fight for Calling

They didn't argue.
They just didn't believe.

And somehow, that was worse.

The Hebrew calls it *qotzer ruach*—
shortness of spirit.

But it felt like I was the one gasping for air.

I stood in the middle of them—carrying words I didn't write—
and they fell like stones into water.

No echo. No ripple.

Just silence.

And behind that silence…
the old voice came rushing back.

"You're not the one."
"You never were."

I told Him again.

"I can't speak."
"I have uncircumcised lips."

It's not just that my tongue trips.
It's that I still feel unclean.
Unworthy.
Unequipped.

Round 3: Moses — The Fight for Calling

I feel like a man dragging a flame he doesn't understand,
trying to set free a people who don't even want to hope anymore.

And I wonder...
why me?

Why now?

Why this way?

But He didn't answer those questions.
Not directly.

He didn't coddle.
He didn't soothe.

He just told me to go again.

"Tell Pharaoh."
"Bring them out."

Like it was that simple.

But maybe it is.

Maybe obedience doesn't wait for everything to feel possible.
Maybe it just keeps moving toward the promise,
even when the path is filled with shadows and no one walks beside
you.

Maybe this is the real fight.

Not the one with Pharaoh.
But the one inside me.

The one that says, *"Keep speaking."*
Even when your voice trembles.
Even when no one listens.
Even when it feels like the Name is too heavy to carry anymore.

I don't know if I'm strong.
But I'm still here.
And I haven't let go yet.

If He's still in this…
then maybe I can go one more round.

The Corner Man Speaks

I never asked you to be eloquent.
I asked you to be faithful.

I never told you it would be easy.
I told you I would be with you.

You stood before Pharaoh,
you spoke when it cost you,
you came back to Me with trembling hands—
and I counted none of it as failure.

I was there the whole time.

You felt their eyes burn with blame.
You watched your words fall flat.
You heard the silence stretch longer than your courage.

But I wasn't measuring your results.

Round 3: Moses — The Fight for Calling

I was watching your heart.

You brought your ache back to Me.
You didn't run.

You asked honest questions.

And that, Moses, is the sound of wrestling.
Not rebellion—relationship.

They couldn't hear you.
Their spirits were crushed.
And yours nearly was too.

But hear Me now:

I have not forgotten the covenant.
I have not misplaced the promise.
And I have not mischosen My servant.

I knew the cracks in your voice.
I knew the weight on your shoulders.
And I still called your name.

Because I knew something you didn't—

That My name would hold
when yours wasn't enough.

You called yourself unworthy.
You called your lips unclean.
But I called you Mine.

And that name is stronger.

Round 3: Moses — The Fight for Calling

You don't have to carry the plan.
Just carry the promise.

You don't have to make them believe.
Just keep speaking what I've spoken.

Because freedom doesn't begin when Pharaoh surrenders—
it begins when you refuse to stop declaring the Name.

So take a breath, son.
You've seen rejection, but you haven't seen redemption yet.
You've been bruised, but you're not broken.

You're My fighter.

And this isn't over.

The Name still wrestles.

And I'm still in your corner.

In This Corner: Moses – Round 3

The Fight for Calling

It didn't happen all at once.

Moses didn't walk out of the wilderness with fire in his bones and
thunder on his lips.
He walked out slowly—limping from the past, second-guessing the call,
wondering if God had made a mistake.

But that's how most of the real ones enter the ring.

Not with bravado.
But with baggage.

This round wasn't about parting seas.
It was about surviving silence.

The kind of silence that sets in after you obey... and nothing changes.
The kind of silence that makes you question whether the fire you saw
still burns,
or if it ever burned at all.

This is where Moses learned what every fighter of faith must learn:

God doesn't test your strength to see if you'll win.
He tests your heart to see if you'll stay.

Calling is not confirmed in the fire.
It's confirmed in the follow-up.
In the return.
In the second breath after failure.

Round 3: Moses — The Fight for Calling

In the voice that says *"I'll go again,"*
even when your lips feel too slow and the crowd is too quiet.

Did you notice?

Moses didn't walk into Egypt with confidence.
He walked in with obedience.

And every time he tried to back out—
every time the people turned,
every time Pharaoh stiffened,
every time the weight got too heavy—
God didn't change the plan.

He just reminded Moses of the Name.

I Am.
I Will.
I Have not forgotten.

That's how you fight when the calling hurts.
You don't wait to feel brave.
You move because the One who called you is still in the corner.

In the end, Moses didn't wrestle with Pharaoh.
He wrestled with himself.
With his past.
With his fears.
With the suffocating pressure of leading people who couldn't breathe.

And still—he showed back up.
He opened his mouth.
He spoke the Name.

Round 3: Moses — The Fight for Calling

And for that...
he stepped into the lineage of those who don't just hear God's
promise—
they carry it.

Bruised.
But blessed.

Because that's who gets the blessing.

Not the ones who glide through.
Not the ones who get it right the first time.

The ones who wrestle.
The ones who stay.
The ones who go back into the ring with a cracked voice and a burning
name.

Round 4

The Fight for Integrity

Job 1:1-22 The Test of the Righteous

📖 *Job 1:1–22*

- Job is blameless and upright
- Satan challenges Job's motives
- Job loses his children and possessions
- Yet he worships: "The Lord gave and the Lord has taken away…"

Job 1:1–22 (NIV)

In the land of Uz there lived a man whose name was Job. This man was blameless and upright; he feared God and shunned evil. He had seven sons and three daughters, and he owned seven thousand sheep, three thousand camels, five hundred yoke of oxen and five hundred donkeys, and had a large number of servants. He was the greatest man among all the people of the East.

His sons used to hold feasts in their homes on their birthdays, and they would invite their three sisters to eat and drink with them. When a period of feasting had run its course, Job would make arrangements for them to be purified. Early in the morning he would sacrifice a burnt offering for each of them, thinking, "Perhaps my children have sinned and cursed God in their hearts." This was Job's regular custom.

One day the angels came to present themselves before the Lord, and Satan also came with them. The Lord said to Satan, "Where have you come from?"

Satan answered the Lord, "From roaming throughout the earth, going back and forth on it."

Round 4: Job – The Fight for Integrity

Then the Lord said to Satan, "Have you considered my servant Job? There is no one on earth like him; he is blameless and upright, a man who fears God and shuns evil."

"Does Job fear God for nothing?" Satan replied. "Have you not put a hedge around him and his household and everything he has? You have blessed the work of his hands, so that his flocks and herds are spread throughout the land. But now stretch out your hand and strike everything he has, and he will surely curse you to your face."

The Lord said to Satan, "Very well, then, everything he has is in your power, but on the man himself do not lay a finger."

Then Satan went out from the presence of the Lord.

One day when Job's sons and daughters were feasting and drinking wine at the oldest brother's house, a messenger came to Job and said, "The oxen were plowing and the donkeys were grazing nearby, and the Sabeans attacked and made off with them. They put the servants to the sword, and I am the only one who has escaped to tell you!"

While he was still speaking, another messenger came and said, "The fire of God fell from the heavens and burned up the sheep and the servants, and I am the only one who has escaped to tell you!"

While he was still speaking, another messenger came and said, "The Chaldeans formed three raiding parties and swept down on your camels and made off with them. They put the servants to the sword, and I am the only one who has escaped to tell you!"

While he was still speaking, yet another messenger came and said, "Your sons and daughters were feasting and drinking wine at the oldest brother's house, when suddenly a mighty wind swept in from the desert and struck the four corners of the house. It collapsed on them and they are dead, and I am the only one who has escaped to tell you!"

At this, Job got up and tore his robe and shaved his head. Then he fell to the ground in worship and said:

"Naked I came from my mother's womb,
and naked I will depart.
The Lord gave and the Lord has taken away;
may the name of the Lord be praised."

In all this, Job did not sin by charging God with wrongdoing.

The Preacher Speaks

Job 1:1–22 – The Test of the Righteous

Before we talk about loss, let's talk about the man.

Job was not a prophet. Not a priest. Not a king. He didn't come from a famous tribe. He didn't carry a title. He simply lived in a land called Uz, beyond the borders of Israel's story—yet somehow, still inside the heart of God's. And what marked him wasn't power or accomplishment. It was character. The text tells us plainly: he was *blameless and upright; he feared God and shunned evil.*

That kind of description doesn't come easily in Scripture. It's not just about morality—it's about alignment. Job lived in a way that echoed God's order. He did what was right when no one was watching. He worshipped in private. He prayed on behalf of his children. After every feast they threw, he would rise early and offer sacrifices, not because he was told to, but because he loved them enough to guard their hearts before God. *Perhaps,* he said, *they have sinned in their hearts. Perhaps they have cursed God without even knowing it.* That small word—*perhaps*—says everything. Job lived carefully. Reverently. Sincerely. And his righteousness was not reactive—it was habitual.

Round 4: Job – The Fight for Integrity

So when we speak of the storm to come, we must not forget this foundation. Job's trial didn't begin because he sinned. It began because he was righteous.

The story then shifts scenes—from the earth to the heavens.

And there, behind a curtain we rarely get to see, a conversation unfolds between the Lord and a figure known in Hebrew as *ha-satan*—literally, "the accuser." Not yet the serpent of Revelation, not the tempter of the Gospels, but a legal adversary in the divine court. He comes among the heavenly council, and God points out His servant Job—not with pride alone, but with affection. "Have you considered my servant Job?" God asks. "There is no one like him on the earth."

But the accuser answers with a question meant to poison the premise: *"Does Job fear God for nothing?"*

It's a chilling accusation—not of Job's actions, but of his motives. The adversary is not denying Job's devotion; he's suggesting it's conditional. He's saying, in essence, *Strip away the blessings, and you'll see the truth. Take away the hedge, and Job will curse You to Your face.*

God does not rebuke him. He does not defend Job with more evidence. Instead, He allows the test. Not because He's unsure of Job's heart—but because He knows the depth of it. He trusts the integrity of His servant enough to permit the storm.

And the storm comes.

Not gradually. Not gently. But in waves of catastrophe so rapid, so disorienting, it's hard to even process.

Round 4: Job – The Fight for Integrity

In the span of a few verses, Job loses everything. Oxen and donkeys are raided. Fire falls from the sky and consumes the sheep. Raiders steal the camels. Servants are slaughtered. And then, the final blow: a wind from the wilderness strikes the home where his children are gathered, and the house collapses. All of them—gone.

Each time, a messenger arrives breathless. Each time, the report ends the same way: *"I alone have escaped to tell you."* It reads like a funeral dirge. A litany of grief. Not one loss, but a cascade—unrelenting and surreal. Most of us would not survive even one of those messages. Job receives four. In a single day.

And yet—this is the part that still steals my breath every time I read it—Job rises. He tears his robe and shaves his head in anguish. He doesn't hide his grief. He doesn't pretend to be fine. But then—he falls to the ground... and worships.

"Naked I came from my mother's womb, and naked I will return.
The Lord gave, and the Lord has taken away;
Blessed be the name of the Lord."

Who says that? Who prays like that—bare, broken, bloodied by loss?

The one who fears God not for gain, but because God is still God.

There's something holy here. Something the accuser cannot understand. Worship that is not a transaction. Faith that is not tethered to outcome. Job does not praise God *because* life is good. He blesses the Name in the ruins of all that was good.

And the last line seals it:

"In all this, Job did not sin by charging God with wrongdoing."

Round 4: Job – The Fight for Integrity

He doesn't explain the suffering. He doesn't justify it. He doesn't pretend to understand it. But he refuses to blame God for it.

That's integrity. That's the fear of the Lord forged in fire.

Before the arguments, before the lament, before the long dialogues and divine speeches, the foundation is laid: Job was righteous before the storm. And he remained righteous inside it.

And this round—this first round—is not won by clarity, or comfort, or answers.

It is won in ashes. With worship. And silence. And faith that doesn't flinch.

The Rabbi Speaks

Job 1:1–22 – A Righteous Man in a Crooked World

Come, my student.
Let us sit beside Job for a while—not to speak, but to listen.
Not to explain suffering, but to reframe it.

You have heard of Job before, I imagine.
Perhaps as a cautionary tale, perhaps as a champion of patience.
But I want you to notice something the text does not rush to tell you:
This is not a story about a sinner punished.
It is a story about a righteous man *tested*.

And in our tradition, that changes everything.

The scroll opens in a land called *Uz*.
Not Jerusalem. Not Zion.

Round 4: Job – The Fight for Integrity

This is a story that unfolds outside the covenant boundaries—
yet strangely, is filled with covenant language.

"There was a man in the land of Uz whose name was Job,
and that man was **blameless** and **upright**, one who **feared God** and
shunned evil."

These four Hebrew phrases are not casual compliments.
They are deliberate echoes of Torah righteousness:

- תָּם (tam) – blameless, whole, complete of heart

- יָשָׁר (yashar) – upright, straight in conduct

- יִרְאֵי אֱלֹהִים (yir'ei Elohim) – one who fears God, a phrase
  found in the Psalms

- סוּר מֵרָע (sur me-ra) – turning away from evil, a wisdom motif

He is not righteous by accident.
He embodies what the sages would call *derekh tzaddikim*—the way of
the righteous.

And then comes the heavenly council scene.

This part troubles many in the West—
God allowing Satan to test a righteous man?
But in our tradition, the *Satan* (הַשָּׂטָן) is not a rogue enemy.
He is a prosecutor. A servant of the court.
One who questions, probes, accuses—
but always under the authority of the Judge.

His question is piercing:

"Does Job fear God for nothing?"

Round 4: Job – The Fight for Integrity

In Hebrew, this is not just suspicion. It's legal challenge.
He implies that Job's righteousness is *purchased*.
That God has surrounded him with a hedge—שׂוּךְ (sukh)—a
protective wall.
Remove the hedge, Satan argues, and Job will curse God to His face.

But the real tension lies here:
What is the purpose of righteousness if it is only upheld by reward?

God's reply is not indifference.
It is confidence.

He allows the test—not to break Job,
but to reveal him.

Not to destroy integrity,
but to display it.

You see, in our tradition, the most righteous are often the ones tested
most severely.
Abraham is tested with Isaac.
Joseph is tested with betrayal.
David is tested with waiting.
And here, Job is tested with loss.

Why?

Because righteousness must be more than a result of reward.
It must be chosen when the rewards are gone.

Now look at Job's response.
Loss after loss, servant after servant, until finally, the unbearable blow:
His children—all of them—are gone.

Round 4: Job – The Fight for Integrity

And what does Job do?

"He arose, tore his robe, shaved his head, and fell to the ground... in worship."

In Hebrew, the tearing of the robe—קָרַע (kara)—is not dramatic flair. It is an act of mourning, still practiced today.
The shaving of the head is a stripping of identity, of status.
And then—he falls in הִשְׁתַּחֲוָה (hishtachavah)—worship, but not with singing.

This is not the worship of the temple.
It is the worship of surrender.

He does not sing. He does not shout.
He *blesses*.

"The Lord gave, and the Lord has taken away;
may the name of the Lord be blessed."
יְהִי שֵׁם יְהוָה מְבֹרָךְ (yehi shem Adonai mevorakh).

That phrase, my student, is still prayed in every Jewish funeral to this day.
Even in the darkest hour, we do not curse the Name.
We bless it.

Not because we understand.
But because He is still worthy.

Job doesn't curse God.
But neither does he suppress grief.

Round 4: Job – The Fight for Integrity

He rips his clothes.
He shaves his head.
He falls to the ground.

And that, too, is holy.

Because integrity is not the absence of emotion.
It is the refusal to sever trust, even when emotion floods the soul.

So remember this:

Job did not win this round by resisting sin.
He won it by refusing to believe that blessing was the only evidence of God's goodness.

And in doing so, he becomes the *first to worship in ashes*—
a priest without a tabernacle,
a mourner who still honors the Name,
a righteous man whose fear of God was not for sale.

The Fighter Speaks

Job 1:1–22 – I'm Still Here

I don't even know how long I've been sitting here.
The dust hasn't settled.
The echo of the last knock still rings in my ears.

They came one after another—
servants, voices, griefs stacked like tombstones.

I tried to track it.
The oxen.
The sheep.
The camels.

Round 4: Job – The Fight for Integrity

The servants.
My children.

My children.

The words felt like fists, each one heavier than the last.
But it was that last blow that buckled my knees.

I tore my robe because I didn't know what else to tear.
I shaved my head because it was the only thing I could still control.
I fell to the ground because the weight of loss was heavier than my
spine could carry.

And I said what I said.

Not because it felt holy.
Not because I wanted to impress God.
But because I needed to say *something* before the silence swallowed me
whole.

"Naked I came from my mother's womb,
and naked I will return."

That's not theology.
That's reality.

I came here with nothing.
And now it seems I'm being returned to nothing.

But still—
still I found myself saying it:

Round 4: Job – The Fight for Integrity

"The Lord gave…
The Lord has taken away…
May the name of the Lord be praised."

What kind of man says that?

I didn't plan it.
Didn't rehearse it.
Didn't mean for it to be anyone's memory of me.

It just came out.

Maybe because… deep down,
I knew this wasn't random.
This wasn't meaningless.

Even if it felt cruel.

I didn't curse Him.
I wanted to.
Oh, I wanted to.

I wanted to scream at the sky and demand why.
I wanted to undo the morning,
rewind the hour,
raise my children from the rubble.

But I didn't curse.

Not because I'm strong.
But because I'm His.

And somehow—somehow—I still believe that He sees me.

Even if I can't see Him right now.

They say I passed the test.

But I wasn't trying to pass anything.

I was just trying to breathe.

And I figured if I was going to breathe again,
it would have to start with worship.
Not because He explained Himself.
But because He didn't walk away.

Not yet.
Not ever.

I'm still here.
And so is He.

And that—somehow—is enough for today.

The Corner Man Speaks

Job 1:1–22 – The Integrity I Knew Was There

I saw him.

Long before Uz knew his name,
before wealth clothed him, before children danced in his fields,
before oxen tread the earth under his yoke—
I saw him.

I knew the shape of his heart.
Not because he was perfect.
But because he was *anchored*.

Round 4: Job – The Fight for Integrity

You might wonder why I said what I said—
"Have you considered my servant Job?"
It was not a gamble.
It was not divine curiosity.
It was confidence.

Not in circumstance.
In **integrity**.

You think integrity is loud.
That it must scream in defense or throw stones at injustice.

But Job's integrity was quiet.
It rose early in the morning to offer sacrifices no one asked for.
It prayed over children who may never have sinned.
It lived as though My presence was always near—even when it wasn't
visible.

So when the accuser came—
when the courtroom assembled and the adversary questioned motive—
I didn't flinch.

Not because I wanted him tested.
But because I knew what the test would reveal.

I never delight in loss.
I am not entertained by ruin.

But there are things this world can only see in fire—
truths that are invisible until the heat peels everything else away.

And in Job…
you saw it, didn't you?

Round 4: Job – The Fight for Integrity

You saw the man who didn't worship Me because he had everything.
You saw the man who worshiped Me when he had *nothing*.

That's the kind of worship that silences accusers.

That's the kind of faith that bruises evil.

That's the kind of righteousness that cannot be bought,
cannot be imitated,
and cannot be burned away.

Yes, Job mourned.
Yes, he tore his robe and shaved his head.
Yes, he wept and trembled and collapsed in ash.

But he also *blessed My name.*

He reminded the heavens—and hell—that integrity is not
circumstantial.

It is covenantal.

And I honored that.
Even in silence.
Even without words.
I stood with him in the ashes.

Because I had known him from the beginning.
And I did not turn away when everything else did.

Job 2:1-13 Ashes and Arguments

📖 *Job 2:1–13*

- Satan strikes again—this time Job's body
- Job's wife urges him to curse God
- Three friends arrive and sit with him in silence
- Grief enters a holy pause before theology speaks

Job 2:1–13 (NIV)

On another day the angels came to present themselves before the Lord, and Satan also came with them to present himself before him.

And the Lord said to Satan, "Where have you come from?"

Satan answered the Lord, "From roaming throughout the earth, going back and forth on it."

Then the Lord said to Satan, "Have you considered my servant Job? There is no one on earth like him; he is blameless and upright, a man who fears God and shuns evil. And he still maintains his integrity, though you incited me against him to ruin him without any reason."

"Skin for skin!" Satan replied. "A man will give all he has for his own life. But now stretch out your hand and strike his flesh and bones, and he will surely curse you to your face."

The Lord said to Satan, "Very well, then, he is in your hands; but you must spare his life."

So Satan went out from the presence of the Lord and afflicted Job with painful sores from the soles of his feet to the crown of his head.

Then Job took a piece of broken pottery and scraped himself with it as he sat among the ashes.

Round 4: Job – The Fight for Integrity

His wife said to him, "Are you still maintaining your integrity? Curse God and die!"

He replied, "You are talking like a foolish woman. Shall we accept good from God, and not trouble?"

In all this, Job did not sin in what he said.

When Job's three friends, Eliphaz the Temanite, Bildad the Shuhite and Zophar the Naamathite, heard about all the troubles that had come upon him, they set out from their homes and met together by agreement to go and sympathize with him and comfort him.

When they saw him from a distance, they could hardly recognize him; they began to weep aloud, and they tore their robes and sprinkled dust on their heads.

Then they sat on the ground with him for seven days and seven nights. No one said a word to him, because they saw how great his suffering was.

The Preacher Speaks

Job 2:1–13 – Ashes and Arguments

There are trials you expect, and there are blows that come after the bell.

Round two opens in heaven, just like the first. Another courtroom. Another wager. But this time, Job isn't merely at risk of losing what he has—he's at risk of losing who he is.

The Accuser returns, still roaming the earth, still searching for cracks in the souls of the righteous. God points again to Job—not with pity, but with pride. "He still maintains his integrity," the Lord says, "though you incited me against him without cause."

Round 4: Job – The Fight for Integrity

But Satan isn't done. He escalates the terms. "Skin for skin," he hisses. "A man will give everything for his own life." Take away the comfort of health, he argues. Strike the body, not just the bank account. Remove the protection of flesh and bone, and even the holiest man will break.

And again, God allows the test—but not without boundaries. "Very well… but you must spare his life."

What follows is unspeakable. Not death. Not war. Not a fall from political power. Just pain. Chronic, relentless, unhealable pain.

Job is covered from head to toe with open sores. We're not told what disease it is. We're simply told it is vile. Agonizing. Humiliating. The kind of affliction that isolates a man from others—and from himself.

And where do we find him? Not in his home. Not surrounded by friends. Not crying out to the heavens.

We find him in the ashes.

He takes a piece of broken pottery and begins to scrape himself. It's grotesque. Primitive. And profoundly human. A man who once bathed in oils and robes is now scraping dead skin with broken clay. Not because he's given up, but because he's trying—however feebly—to stay alive.

And then the voice closest to him speaks.

His wife, once a partner in blessing, becomes a mirror of despair. "Are you still holding on to your integrity?" she asks. "Curse God and die."

Round 4: Job – The Fight for Integrity

We should not be too hard on her. She has lost children too. She has watched her husband's body decay. She has no prophetic perspective. All she sees is a man unraveling, and a God who seems silent.

But Job, in his pain, does not return her words with cruelty. He simply says, "You're speaking like a foolish woman. Shall we accept good from God and not trouble?"

This is not arrogance. It's clarity. Job refuses to make his faith conditional. He still doesn't accuse God. He still doesn't sin with his lips.

And heaven, though quiet, is watching.

Then, three friends arrive. Eliphaz, Bildad, Zophar. They've heard of his suffering. They've left their homes. And when they see him from a distance, they don't recognize him.

That line cuts deep.

They've known him for years—but suffering has disfigured him. And they do the only thing they know to do: they tear their robes, they throw dust on their heads, and they sit with him.

For seven days and seven nights, they say nothing.

No advice. No theology. No false comfort.

Just silence.

Because they see that Job's suffering is too great for words.

Round 4: Job – The Fight for Integrity

This is the space between theology and empathy. The holy pause. The ash-covered silence that understands sometimes presence is more powerful than answers.

What comes next in the story will be speeches and debates, arguments and accusations. But here, for just one moment, there is something sacred.

Three friends. One mourner. And a week of wordless witness.

This isn't the climax. It's the interlude.

But in the life of the righteous, sometimes the most faithful thing you can do... is sit in the ashes and say nothing at all.

The Rabbi Speaks

Job 2:1–13 – The Wounds That Worship

Come close now. This moment is heavy.
The scroll still weeps with ashes, and the parchment smells of pain.

But I want you to see what the Western world often misses:
This chapter isn't about God abandoning Job.
It's about God trusting him again.

Yes, *again*.

The heavenly court is back in session.
And the *satan*—the adversary, the challenger—returns.

"From roaming throughout the earth," he says,
"going back and forth on it."

Round 4: Job – The Fight for Integrity

He is not idle. He is searching.
But not just for sin. For motive.
For anyone who does good—for the wrong reasons.

And once again, the Holy One brings up Job.
Not because He enjoys the test.
But because He believes in His servant.

Listen to the words carefully:

"He still maintains his integrity, though you incited Me against him for no reason."

In Hebrew:
וְעֹדֶנּוּ מַחֲזִיק בְּתֻמָּתוֹ (v'odennu machazik b'tummato) —
"He still clings to his integrity."

The word תֻּמָּה (tummah) comes from תָּם (tam)—blameless, whole.
This is not just moral restraint.
This is *wholeness* under pressure.
Integrity that *holds* when everything else falls.

Then the adversary sharpens the blade:

"Skin for skin… strike his flesh, and he will surely curse You to Your face."

But this is not just a test of endurance.
It is a test of *embodiment*.

Will Job still fear God when his very body turns against him?

And God permits it—on one condition:
"Spare his life."

Round 4: Job – The Fight for Integrity

Do you see it?

Even in trial, God sets a boundary.
The adversary may afflict, but he may not annihilate.

Because suffering, in our tradition, is not a license for destruction.
It is a furnace that refines—never a fire that consumes.

Now look at Job.

Covered in boils from foot to crown.
No ointments. No physician. No relief.
Just shards of pottery and a heap of ashes.

And yet, even here, something sacred is happening.

"He sat among the ashes."

In Hebrew: בָּאֵפֶר (ba'efer) — the same word used in sacrificial rituals.
The ashes of the altar.
The residue of offering.

Job isn't just mourning.
He's becoming the offering.

Not to appease God.
But to remain with Him.

He scrapes his sores not because he despairs—
but because he still cares.

A man with no hope doesn't scrape.
He surrenders.

But Job is still *engaged*.

Round 4: Job – The Fight for Integrity

Even in agony, he clings.

Now, his wife speaks.
And you must not judge her too quickly.
She, too, has lost children.
She, too, has watched her home fall into ruin.

She is not Job's enemy.
She is grief given voice.

"Curse God and die," she says.

In Hebrew, the word is בָּרֵךְ (barekh)—strangely, the word for "bless."
Why? Because in ancient euphemism, to "bless" God in this context
means to say the unspeakable.

It's the language of despair cloaked in religious terms.

But Job replies gently,
"Shall we receive good from God, and not also evil?"

He doesn't deny the pain.
He refuses to weaponize it.

And still, the text says:

"In all this, Job did not sin with his lips."

Then come the friends.

Three men—Eliphaz, Bildad, Zophar—arrive not with doctrine, but
with *presence*.

Round 4: Job – The Fight for Integrity

And when they see Job, they weep.
They tear their clothes.
They sit with him.

Seven days.
Seven nights.
Not a word spoken.

In the Hebrew mind, this is not silence by default.
It is silence by design.

This is *shivah*—the mourning period still observed in Jewish tradition.
When someone is suffering, you do not speak until they speak first.
You wait. You grieve with your body.
Because sometimes, theology is a poor substitute for empathy.

And so I ask you:

Can you sit with those who suffer—without reaching for explanations?
Can you worship with those who bleed—without quoting promises too soon?

In Job's silence, there is wisdom.
In his wife's anguish, there is honesty.
And in his friends' stillness—before their speeches—there is something holy.

Before the arguments begin…
there is ashes.

And the God of Abraham is still there,
even in the dust.

The Fighter Speaks

Round 4: Job – The Fight for Integrity

Job 2:1–13 – I Am Still in This Body

My hands tremble.
Not from fear—but from fever.
The sores won't stop spreading.
The skin on my back itches like madness, but when I reach for it, it
tears.

There's no word for this.
No prayer that fits.
Just pain.
Constant.
Throbbing.
Like my body's turned against me one nerve at a time.

I don't even know how long I've been out here in the ashes.
The ground is cold.
The sky is far.
And I've lost track of where my voice ends and the silence begins.

I scraped my skin today with broken clay.
Not because it helped—
but because it was all I had.

The man I was—
the man people used to admire—
he's somewhere under this sickness.
Or maybe he isn't.

What's left of me?

A breath.
A question.
A flicker of belief so small I'm ashamed to name it.

My wife stood over me.

She didn't shout.
She didn't scream.
She just looked at me like a man already dead and asked me to finish the job.

"Curse God and die."

I wanted to scream.
Not at her.
But at the ache that stole her hope.
She's hurting too.
She's just lost the will to pretend.

But I'm not done yet.

I told her:

"Shall we accept good from God, and not trouble?"

It didn't come from courage.
It came from confusion.
From the little corner of me that still believes in covenant—
even when it feels like the covenant has forgotten me.

And now they've come.
My friends.

They didn't speak.
Not one of them.
Just sat down beside me.

Round 4: Job – The Fight for Integrity

Dust in their hair.
Tears in their eyes.

They looked at me like they didn't recognize me—
and maybe they didn't.

Because grief changes a man.
Suffering alters the shape of your soul.
Even I don't recognize my voice anymore.

But there's something about this silence—
seven days of it—
that feels strangely holy.

Like maybe God is watching too.
Not with judgment.
Not with lightning.

Just watching.

Just… here.

I am not asking for answers.

I'm just trying to breathe through the burning.
To stay tethered to a God I can no longer feel.

This isn't faith because I understand.
It's faith because I refuse to leave.

I may be in the ashes—
but I'm still in this fight.

The Corner Man Speaks

Job 2:1–13 – The Space Between Words

I watched as the Accuser prowled back into My court,
smirking, restless, as if he had found the crack I missed.

"Skin for skin," he said.
"Strike his flesh, and even your servant will curse you."

But I knew what the Accuser did not.

Job was not worshiping Me for what I gave.
He was holding onto Me for who I am.

So I permitted the wound, but not the death.
I allowed the test, but not the end.

That's what love does when it knows what it placed inside a man—
when it knows the weight of glory is greater than the weight of dust.

I saw Job sit in the ashes.
Not because he lost hope,
but because he still believed it meant something to stay close to the
place where fire had fallen.

He scraped his wounds with broken pottery—
but he never turned his face from Me.

His wife lost her breath,
and her words came out like shattered glass.
But Job's reply...
it was not cold.
It was honest.
Measured.
Full of pain, but not betrayal.

Round 4: Job – The Fight for Integrity

"Shall we accept good from God, and not trouble?"

He didn't know the full story.
He didn't know that I had just defended his name before the hosts of heaven.
He didn't see Me hold the line when darkness wanted more.

But he still honored Me with his mouth.

Then his friends came.

They sat.
They wept.
They said nothing.

And I was in that silence.

Don't miss that.

I was in the torn robes.
In the dust on their heads.
In the space between the sobs.

Because when grief is too deep for words,
I do not rush to fill it.
I enter it.

That is how I honor the righteous—
not by preventing the pain,
but by joining them in it.

And though Job could not see Me,
I was there.

Round 4: Job – The Fight for Integrity

Not explaining.
Not defending.

Just *there*.

In the ashes.
In the scraping.
In the silence.

Because the ones who still sit in the dust with Me—
those are the ones I trust to carry My name
when the world no longer makes sense.

Job 3:1-26 Let the Day Perish

Job 3:1–26

- Job curses the day of his birth
- He does not curse God—but he does curse his own existence
- Darkness becomes a form of prayer

Job 3:1–26 (NIV)

After this, Job opened his mouth and cursed the day of his birth. He said:

"May the day of my birth perish,
and the night that said, 'A boy is conceived!'
That day—may it turn to darkness;
may God above not care about it;
may no light shine on it.

May gloom and utter darkness claim it once more;
may a cloud settle over it;
may blackness overwhelm it.

That night—may thick darkness seize it;
may it not be included among the days of the year
nor be entered in any of the months.

May that night be barren;
may no shout of joy be heard in it.
May those who curse days curse that day,
those who are ready to rouse Leviathan.

May its morning stars become dark;
may it wait for daylight in vain

and not see the first rays of dawn,
for it did not shut the doors of the womb on me
to hide trouble from my eyes.

Why did I not perish at birth,
and die as I came from the womb?
Why were there knees to receive me
and breasts that I might be nursed?

For now I would be lying down in peace;
I would be asleep and at rest
with kings and rulers of the earth,
who built for themselves places now lying in ruins,
with princes who had gold,
who filled their houses with silver.

Or why was I not hidden away in the ground like a stillborn child,
like an infant who never saw the light of day?

There the wicked cease from turmoil,
and there the weary are at rest.

Captives also enjoy their ease;
they no longer hear the slave driver's shout.

The small and the great are there,
and the slaves are freed from their owners.

Why is life given to those in misery,
and life to the bitter of soul,
to those who long for death that does not come,
who search for it more than for hidden treasure,
who are filled with gladness
and rejoice when they reach the grave?

Round 4: Job – The Fight for Integrity

Why is life given to a man
whose way is hidden,
whom God has hedged in?

For sighing has become my daily food;
my groans pour out like water.
What I feared has come upon me;
what I dreaded has happened to me.
I have no peace, no quietness;
I have no rest, but only turmoil."

The Preacher Speaks

Job 3:1–26 – Let the Day Perish

It takes seven days of silence before Job opens his mouth.
Seven days in the ashes.
Seven days of no resolution, no rescue, no divine reply.

And then the dam breaks.
But not in praise.
Not in strength.
Not even in prayer.

Job opens his mouth and speaks the one thing we pretend the
righteous never say:

"Let the day of my birth perish."

He doesn't curse God.
He curses himself.
His birthday.
His beginning.

Let's pause here.

Round 4: Job – The Fight for Integrity

This is not the moment some of us wanted.
We wanted a spiritual titan to rise from the rubble with words of gold and steel.
But Job doesn't preach. He doesn't quote scripture. He doesn't summon strength.

He groans.

He curses the day the umbilical cord was cut.
He weeps over the night his mother conceived him.
He asks for darkness to swallow up the memory of his life before it ever began.

This isn't heresy. It's honesty.

He says, *"May that day be barren… may no light shine on it… may those who curse days curse it… may it not be counted among the days of the year."*

This is not poetic exaggeration.
This is a man past the point of politeness.
He's not asking for healing—he's wishing he never existed.

Have you ever been there?

Not suicidal. Just soul-empty.
Not angry. Just undone.

Job's not asking for death because he's weak.
He's asking for erasure because he feels his life has become a burden to God, to others, to himself.

And still, he doesn't sin.
Still, he doesn't curse the name of the Lord.
Still, he lifts his eyes toward the heavens—even if just to ask why they ever opened over him.

The preachers of comfort rarely know what to do with Job 3.

There's no moral here. No tidy resolution. No bow to wrap around this ash heap.

Only questions.

"Why did I not perish at birth?"
"Why was I received at the breast?"
"Why is life given to those in misery?"
"Why is life given to the bitter of soul?"

These are not rhetorical. They are cries.
They come from a man who once had everything, and now would settle for nothing—just to make the pain stop.

But here's what I want you to see:

Even in his darkest moment, Job is still speaking.
He hasn't shut down.
He hasn't gone silent.
He hasn't turned his face fully away.

This is faith with a limp.
Worship through a scream.

And somewhere, in the divine silence, God is still listening.

Not because Job says the right things.
But because Job dares to say *real* things.

This is what integrity looks like in the dark.

Round 4: Job – The Fight for Integrity

It's not strength.
It's not serenity.

It's *truth*.

Job 3 is not a sermon.
It's a psalm in ashes.

And if you've ever wanted to cry out, *"Let the day perish…"*
you're in good company.

Because the fighters who refuse to fake it—
are the ones I believe God still fights for.

The Rabbi Speaks

Job 3:1–26 – The Darkness That Speaks

Pull your chair closer. You will not understand this passage if you read it with Western eyes.

You see despair.
You hear depression.
You think, *This can't be righteous.*

But in the East, we know the value of darkness.
We do not rush to erase it.
We do not fear its silence.
We honor it, because God has spoken from it before.

"And God said, 'Let there be light'—and there was light."
But before that?
Darkness was over the surface of the deep.

Round 4: Job – The Fight for Integrity

In Hebrew: חֹשֶׁךְ עַל־פְּנֵי תְהוֹם (choshekh al-p'nei tehom)
Darkness over the face of the deep.

Tehom—the deep, the abyss.
The same abyss Job now stares into.

But don't look away.
Because Job is not sinning.
He is praying.
Yes, cursing the day of his birth is a form of prayer in Hebrew tradition.
It's the prayer of the honest. The undone. The overwhelmed.

Job doesn't curse God.
He curses the **day**.
In Hebrew, he says:

יֹאבַד יוֹם אִוָּלֶד בּוֹ (yo'vad yom ivvaled bo)
Let the day perish on which I was born.

He's not denying God.
He's collapsing before Him.

There is a difference.

And then comes the poetry—dark, sharp, relentless.

Job calls for that day to vanish from the calendar:

"May it not be included among the days of the year…"

He calls for those who curse days—likely ancient sorcerers or lamenters—to invoke Leviathan to consume the memory of it.

Round 4: Job – The Fight for Integrity

"May those who curse days… rouse Leviathan."

In ancient Hebrew lore, **Leviathan** is not just a sea monster.
It is *chaos itself.*
To rouse Leviathan is to invite the undoing of order.

Why?

Because Job no longer trusts the order.
He has kept the law. He has done no evil.
And yet his world has unraveled.

He is not cursing the Creator.
He's asking whether chaos was the truth all along.

"Why was I not hidden like a stillborn child?"
"Why is life given to those who long for death?"

These are not philosophical questions.
They are personal indictments against a system that once promised blessing for obedience.

And in Job's world—our world—that system has cracked.

But do not think this is faithlessness.
No, this is **emunah**—a faith that clings through confusion.

In Hebrew, אֱמוּנָה (emunah) does not mean belief without doubt.
It means *steadfastness. Loyalty.*
It means not letting go of the covenant even when the covenant seems to have let go of you.

And what of the fear?

Round 4: Job – The Fight for Integrity

"What I feared has come upon me."

This verse haunts many.
Some say it implies that Job's dread somehow brought this on himself.

But no. That is not how we read it.

In the Hebrew, this is not blame.
It is grief.

כִּי פַחַד פָּחַדְתִּי וַיֶּאֱתֵנִי (ki pachad pachad'ti vaye'eteni)
What I dreaded has overtaken me.

Job is saying: *I saw this in my nightmares... and now I'm living it.*

That's not guilt.
That's trauma.

So what does it mean, all this darkness?

In our tradition, darkness is not the opposite of God's presence.
It is often the container of it.

"The Lord dwells in thick darkness." (1 Kings 8:12)

יְהוָה אָמַר לִשְׁכֹּן בָּעֲרָפֶל (Adonai amar lishkon ba'arafel)
The Lord said He would dwell in the thick cloud.

Sometimes, the darkness is not abandonment.
It is invitation.

An invitation to speak.
To cry.
To curse the day—
and still, somehow,
to stay.

Let Western religion rush to rescue.
Let Eastern wisdom remind you:
There is sacred ground beneath the ash heap.

And the one who dares to weep there is not lost.
He is held.

"This is not a breakdown—it's a holy lament.
Job does not curse God; he curses the silence between what he
believed and what he now sees.
In our tradition, to cry out is not rebellion—it is relationship.
He does not walk away.
He stays.
And that… is faith."

The Fighter Speaks

Job 3:1–26 – I Spoke Because the Silence Was Killing Me

Seven days I held it in.

Seven days I sat in the ash heap,
trying to remember how to breathe,
how to pray,
how to be.

And I couldn't do it anymore.

I didn't curse God.
But I couldn't keep pretending I was okay.
I couldn't pretend the pain made sense,
or that I still believed every answer I used to preach.

Round 4: Job – The Fight for Integrity

So I opened my mouth and I spoke.
Not to be strong.
Not to impress.
But because the silence was heavier than the grief.

"Let the day of my birth perish."

I don't regret saying it.
I needed to say it.
To name the ache.
To look the darkness in the eye and admit it had gotten inside me.

I used to light candles on my birthday.
Now I want that day gone.
Off the calendar.
Erased from the story.

I'm not asking to die.
I'm asking why I ever lived—
if this was where the path was leading.

I said things some people would call heresy.
But I didn't curse Him.
I didn't walk away.
I just wept from within the covenant.

Because here's the thing:

If God really formed me,
then He can handle the sound of me breaking.

If He knit me together,
then He already knows the threads that are unraveling.

I didn't ask for this fight.
Didn't train for it.
Didn't provoke it.

But I'm here.
Breathing in dust.
Sifting through memories.
Trying to remember the sound of my children's laughter
without breaking in half.

I'm not okay.
But I'm still here.
And I still have something to say.

Even if that something is:

"Where are You?"

I haven't given up on God.

I've just lost the version of Him I used to know.

And maybe…
just maybe…
that's part of the fight.

The Corner Man Speaks

Job 3:1–26 – I Didn't Flinch When He Cursed the Day

I didn't look away when Job opened his mouth.
I didn't stop him.

Round 4: Job – The Fight for Integrity

Didn't hush him.
Didn't rebuke him for cursing the day he was born.

I listened.

Because sometimes grief has no filter.
And when a righteous man weeps like this,
he isn't walking away from Me—
he's collapsing into Me.

He said it clearly:

"Let the day of my birth perish…"

And I didn't erase those words.
I wrote them down.

Right there in My book.

Because lament is not the opposite of faith—
it's the evidence of it.

Only those who believe I'm still listening
bother to cry out in the dark.

He asked questions he could not answer.

Why was I born?
Why did You let me live?
Why is life given to those in misery?

He didn't ask to be rescued.
He asked to be understood.

Round 4: Job – The Fight for Integrity

And I understood.

Not because I needed to hear the words—
but because *he* needed to know he could say them.

That's what the covenant is.
Not a contract of silence.
But a bond that holds when everything else breaks.

He imagined Leviathan devouring the day.
He invited chaos to undo the order.
He wondered if maybe darkness was truer than light.

And still…
he never let go of My name.

He never turned to another god.
Never traded Me in for comfort.

Even when he couldn't find Me,
he still spoke toward Me.

And that…
that is the kind of honesty I honor.

Job's curse of the day was not blasphemy.
It was a battle cry.

Because even a soul crushed under sorrow
can still choose to speak instead of staying silent.

And I count that as worship.

Round 4: Job – The Fight for Integrity

He doesn't know it yet,
but this lament will echo in generations to come.
It will become part of sacred scripture.
A psalm in prose.
A prayer from the pit.

Because I don't just dwell in light.
I dwell in the thick darkness too.

And I don't just bless the ones who sing.
I bless the ones who scream.

Job 38:1- Words Without Knowledge

Job 38:1–40:2

- God finally responds—but not with answers
- "Where were you when I laid the earth's foundation?"
- Job is confronted not with explanation, but with awe

The Lord Speaks

Then the Lord spoke to Job out of the storm. He said:

"Who is this that obscures my plans
with words without knowledge?
Brace yourself like a man;
I will question you,
and you shall answer me.

"Where were you when I laid the earth's foundation?
Tell me, if you understand.
Who marked off its dimensions? Surely you know!
Who stretched a measuring line across it?
On what were its footings set,
or who laid its cornerstone—
while the morning stars sang together
and all the angels shouted for joy?

"Who shut up the sea behind doors
when it burst forth from the womb,
when I made the clouds its garment
and wrapped it in thick darkness,
when I fixed limits for it
and set its doors and bars in place,

when I said, 'This far you may come and no farther;
here is where your proud waves halt'?

"Have you ever given orders to the morning,
or shown the dawn its place,
that it might take the earth by the edges
and shake the wicked out of it?
The earth takes shape like clay under a seal;
its features stand out like those of a garment.
The wicked are denied their light,
and their upraised arm is broken.

"Have you journeyed to the springs of the sea
or walked in the recesses of the deep?
Have the gates of death been shown to you?
Have you seen the gates of the deepest darkness?
Have you comprehended the vast expanses of the earth?
Tell me, if you know all this.

"What is the way to the abode of light?
And where does darkness reside?
Can you take them to their places?
Do you know the paths to their dwellings?
Surely you know, for you were already born!
You have lived so many years!

(This divine monologue continues across two chapters. Highlights continue below.)

"Have you entered the storehouses of the snow
or seen the storehouses of the hail,
which I reserve for times of trouble,
for days of war and battle?

"Do you know the laws of the heavens?
Can you set up God's dominion over the earth?

Round 4: Job – The Fight for Integrity

"Can you raise your voice to the clouds
and cover yourself with a flood of water?
Do you send the lightning bolts on their way?
Do they report to you, 'Here we are'?

"Do you give the horse its strength
or clothe its neck with a flowing mane?

"Does the hawk take flight by your wisdom
and spread its wings toward the south?
Does the eagle soar at your command
and build its nest on high?"

Job 40:1–2 (NIV)

The Lord said to Job:
"Will the one who contends with the Almighty correct him?
Let him who accuses God answer him!"

The Preacher Speaks

Job 38:1–40:2 – When God Asks the Questions

It had been a long silence.

Thirty-five chapters of human processing.
Of sitting with suffering, wrestling with theology, and choking on the weight of loss.
Job had buried his children, watched his wealth turn to dust, and scraped boils from his body with a broken piece of pottery.
He had endured bad advice and worse comfort.
And after all that, after every breath of human wisdom had dried up in the desert wind… God finally speaks.

But not softly. Not in the calm. Not in the resolution.

Round 4: Job – The Fight for Integrity

He speaks from the storm.

And sometimes, so does He still.

The first words from heaven are not explanations—they are questions. Dozens of them. Each one echoing through the whirlwind like thunder.

"Who is this that darkens My counsel with words without knowledge?"
"Where were you when I laid the earth's foundation?"
"Can you bind the chains of the Pleiades?"
"Do you send the lightning bolts on their way?"

To some, it might sound like scolding. But if you've ever grieved deeply—if you've ever wept until your voice broke—then you know: there's a kind of comfort that comes only when the silence finally breaks, even if the voice isn't gentle.

This isn't a cold lecture.
It's a recalibration.
God is reintroducing Himself—not as the subject of Job's arguments, but as the Sovereign who cannot be reduced to them.

Let's bring it closer to home.

When you lose everything, you look for reasons. When the job disappears, the child wanders, the test result comes back terminal, or your spouse walks out… you start to flip through every page of your life looking for the line where it all went wrong. You cry out like Job, not just in pain but in protest. You say things you wouldn't say in Sunday school. You ask questions you didn't know were allowed.

And heaven seems quiet.

Round 4: Job – The Fight for Integrity

Then, sometimes, a storm rolls in—not of tragedy, but of *truth*.
It isn't always the answer we wanted. But it's God, showing up.

That's what happened to Job.
That's what still happens to us.

God doesn't show Job a blueprint.
He shows him the night sky.
He points to the storehouses of snow, the migration of birds, the untamed strength of wild animals.
He overwhelms him with the sheer immensity of creation.
Why?

Because Job's world had gotten so small.
And that's what pain does—it collapses the horizon.
Grief turns your soul into a room with no windows.

So God blows the walls out.

He expands Job's field of vision—not to dismiss his suffering, but to remind him of the larger story he still belongs to.

And maybe that's the word some of us need today.

When all you can see is the pain, the loss, the unfairness—He speaks from the whirlwind not to mock your suffering, but to draw you into awe.

He doesn't give Job a manual.
He gives him a *mystery*.
He says, in essence, *"You are not the center of this—but you are not forgotten by it, either."*

One of the hardest things about suffering in modern life is how isolated it feels. We carry grief in sterile hospital rooms and empty bank accounts. We suffer in secret, scrolling through curated lives on social media while wondering if God still hears the silence under our smiles.

Job's story reminds us that God's silence is not absence.
And His storm is not rejection.
It is sometimes His *entrance*.

The preacher in me has to say this plainly:
If you're walking through your own whirlwind—
don't fear the questions.
Don't fear the voice that disrupts your logic.
Don't assume the storm is punishment.

It may just be the sound of your Redeemer drawing near.

And He's not coming with all the answers.

He's coming with Himself.

The Rabbi Speaks
Job 38:1–40:2 – The Voice from the Whirlwind

Come. Sit beside me beneath the open sky. Let the winds stir and the dust rise. We will not run from it. We will read from within it.

You have heard Job's cries.
You have watched him unravel—his grief, his questions, his dignity hanging by a thread.
But now, something ancient breaks the silence.

"Then the LORD answered Job **from the whirlwind**…"

Round 4: Job – The Fight for Integrity

In Hebrew, the word is *sə'ārāh* (סְעָרָה)—a tempest, a storm, a swirling chaos.
It is the same type of storm that will later carry Elijah to heaven.
The same force that once descended on Sinai.
This is not a destructive storm.
It is a **divine arrival**.

And then… the questions begin. Seventy-seven of them.
God speaks—but not to explain.
He speaks to **summon**.
Not to justify Himself—but to reorient Job.

"Where were you when I laid the foundations of the earth?"
"Do you know where the mountain goats give birth?"
"Can you leash the Leviathan?"

These are not insults. They are invitations.
Each question expands Job's collapsed world.
Grief had become his only horizon.
Pain had blurred the edges of all things.

So God widens the frame.
Not to diminish Job's suffering—but to **de-center** it.
To lift his gaze to the stars, the sea, the storm, the wild and the wondrous.

Let me teach you something precious.

In Hebrew, wisdom is *ḥokhmah* (חָכְמָה)—not merely knowledge, but **woven order**, a kind of sacred architecture of the universe.
God is showing Job not His power to punish, but His craftsmanship to sustain.

Round 4: Job – The Fight for Integrity

He is saying, in essence:
"You see the thread. I see the tapestry."

Now lean in. Let me show you the moment that takes my breath away every time I read it.

הֲרֹב עִם־שַׁדַּי יִסּוֹר

Ha-rov im Shaddai yissor
"Shall the one wrestling with Shaddai still instruct Him?"

Did you hear that?

The word used here is **רֹב** (*rav*)—from *riv*, meaning to strive, contend, plead, argue, fight.

God calls Job a **wrestler.**

And He does not rebuke him for it.
He does not call him faithless.
He does not cast him out.

He names the **wrestling**. And He stays in it.

In our tradition, to wrestle with God is not rebellion—it is relationship. The name of our people, *Israel*, comes from a night fight with a Divine Stranger.
Jacob did not win by strength. He won by *not letting go*.

And now Job is folded into that lineage.
The lineage of those who cry out and stay.
Those who bleed in the presence of the Holy but refuse to turn away.

Round 4: Job – The Fight for Integrity

This is the sacred paradox:
That the Almighty does not punish the one who struggles—
He blesses him.

The Western world often seeks to resolve pain with answers.
But in the East, and in the soul of Torah, we are taught that some pain
is not to be solved—but to be **held**.
And not held alone.

This moment is not about Job's smallness.
It is about God's **nearness**.

He comes in the storm—not to lecture, but to speak.
Not to fix, but to **be known**.

So take heart, dear student.

If you find yourself contending with the Almighty,
if your prayers feel more like protests,
if your wounds speak louder than your theology—

You may be closer to the blessing than you think.

Because the One in the whirlwind still answers wrestlers by name.
And the name He gives is never rejection.

It is always, always… *beloved.*

The Fighter Speaks
Job 38:1–40:2 – In the Whirlwind

I wanted answers.
I wanted a reason for the graves I dug.

Round 4: Job – The Fight for Integrity

For the boils on my skin.
For the silence that echoed louder than any comfort.

I thought I was ready for justice.
Turns out, I was only ready for revenge.

And then—He came.
Not in the way I expected.
Not with an apology or a defense.
Not with the soft tones of reassurance.
But with a storm.

The sky cracked open like the earth did when my children were buried.
And out of it, He spoke.

I braced myself.
I had rehearsed my argument like a man on trial.
But when I heard His voice, my script turned to ash.
Because what do you say to the One who hung Orion?
To the One who stores the snow and sends the lightning bolts like arrows from a quiver?

He didn't scold me.
But He didn't coddle me either.
He overwhelmed me—with wonder.
He buried my why beneath a hundred better questions.

There was one line I can't shake.
He called me *rav*—a **wrestler**.

Me.

Not rebel.
Not fool.
Not accuser.
Wrestler.

And I realized… He never walked away from me.
Even when I was throwing words like fists into the sky.
Even when my prayers bled into curses.
He stayed.

He spoke.

He showed me Leviathan.
He reminded me that there are wild things in this world that cannot be tamed, only trusted to Him.

Maybe I am one of those things.

I didn't get an explanation.
I got a voice.

I didn't get justice.
I got a presence.

And somehow… I can live with that.

Because if I can still feel Him—
even here, in the ashes,
then I haven't lost everything.

Maybe I've lost the God I used to understand.
But I've met the One who *sees me* in the whirlwind.
And I can hold on to that.

The Corner Man Speaks
Job 38:1–40:2 – Between the Bell and the Breath

Round 4: Job – The Fight for Integrity

You held your breath when heaven went silent.
You thought silence meant absence.
But I was there the whole time—waiting until your strength ran out…
so your soul could speak.

You thought you needed answers.
But answers are fragile things.
They crumble in the heat of suffering.

You didn't need a reason.
You needed a **revelation**.

So I came in the storm.
Not to frighten you, but to show you what has always been true:
That My voice is bigger than your wounds,
and My presence deeper than your pain.

You called me Judge.
But I was your Witness.
You called me Distant.
But I was your Dust and your Wind.

I did not come to debate.
I came to **remind**.

Remind you that I laid the foundations of the earth…
And I laid My hand on your shoulder before your first breath.

You've been fighting Me—but not away from Me.
And that makes all the difference.

Because I do not turn away wrestlers.
I **bless** them.

And when the storm clears, and the ache remains,
you'll still be standing.

Round 4: Job – The Fight for Integrity

Not because you won,
but because you stayed.

And I'll still be here—
in the ashes,
in the silence,
in the whirlwind—
whispering:

"You are not alone."

Job 42:1-17 Dust and Restoration

📖 *Job 42:1–17*

- Job repents—not of sin, but of smallness
- God rebukes the friends but honors Job's honesty
- Job's fortunes are restored
- But he walks out of the ashes with a new kind of wisdom

Then Job replied to the Lord:

"I know that you can do all things;
no purpose of yours can be thwarted.
You asked, 'Who is this that obscures my plans without
knowledge?'
Surely I spoke of things I did not understand,
things too wonderful for me to know.
You said, 'Listen now, and I will speak;
I will question you,
and you shall answer me.'
My ears had heard of you
but now my eyes have seen you.
Therefore I despise myself
and repent in dust and ashes."

After the Lord had said these things to Job,
he said to Eliphaz the Temanite:
"I am angry with you and your two friends,
because you have not spoken the truth about me,
as my servant Job has.
So now take seven bulls and seven rams
and go to my servant Job
and sacrifice a burnt offering for yourselves.
My servant Job will pray for you,
and I will accept his prayer
and not deal with you according to your folly.

Round 4: Job – The Fight for Integrity

You have not spoken the truth about me,
as my servant Job has."

So Eliphaz the Temanite, Bildad the Shuhite, and Zophar the Naamathite
did what the Lord told them;
and the Lord accepted Job's prayer.

After Job had prayed for his friends,
the Lord restored his fortunes
and gave him twice as much as he had before.
All his brothers and sisters
and everyone who had known him before
came and ate with him in his house.
They comforted and consoled him
over all the trouble the Lord had brought on him,
and each one gave him a piece of silver and a gold ring.

The Lord blessed the latter part of Job's life more than the former part.
He had fourteen thousand sheep, six thousand camels,
a thousand yoke of oxen and a thousand donkeys.
And he also had seven sons and three daughters.
The first daughter he named Jemimah,
the second Keziah,
and the third Keren-Happuch.
Nowhere in all the land
were there found women as beautiful as Job's daughters,
and their father granted them an inheritance
along with their brothers.

After this, Job lived a hundred and forty years;
he saw his children and their children to the fourth generation.
And so Job died, an old man and full of years.

The Preacher Speaks

Round 4: Job – The Fight for Integrity

The storm has passed.
The ashes are still on the ground, but the whirlwind has gone quiet.
And now, Job speaks.

But notice what he doesn't say.
He doesn't say, "Now I understand everything."
He doesn't say, "I must have deserved this."
He doesn't even say, "Thank you for explaining."

What he does say is this:

"Surely I spoke of things I did not understand,
things too wonderful for me to know."

This isn't a confession of wrongdoing—it's a confession of awe.
Job hasn't solved anything. No mystery has been unraveled.
But something has shifted. His soul is no longer demanding answers;
it's bowing before something far bigger than his suffering: the presence
of God.

He's been humbled, yes—but not humiliated.
He's not silenced by guilt—he's quieted by glory.
And that distinction matters.

Throughout the story, Job was demanding justice. His friends were
defending doctrine.
But in the end, it wasn't about proving who was right.
It was about who stayed honest—who stayed in the relationship.

And Job did.

God says it plainly:

"You have not spoken the truth about me, as my servant Job has."

Round 4: Job – The Fight for Integrity

Let that sink in.
The man who cried out, who wept and raged and questioned God—
that's the one God calls *faithful*.
Not the ones who wrapped pain in tidy theological bows.

Why?
Because Job never walked away.

Even in grief.
Even in confusion.
Even when heaven felt silent and unfair.

He kept talking.
He kept reaching.
He kept showing up in the conversation.

And to God, that counts as righteousness.

Then something remarkable happens.
God tells Job to pray for his friends.

He doesn't ask him to rebuke them.
He doesn't allow him to feel vindicated.
He invites Job to **intercede**.

And Job does.

That's the fruit of integrity—not pride, but compassion.
Not revenge, but priesthood.

Job becomes the one who carries others through the very storm he just survived.

Round 4: Job – The Fight for Integrity

But even here, the restoration isn't a reset button.
It doesn't erase what happened.
It doesn't pretend the suffering didn't matter.

It simply says:

You're still mine.
You're still standing.
And I still have life to give you.

"The Lord blessed the latter part of Job's life more than the former…"

And yet, we know the real blessing wasn't the wealth or the years.
It was that Job had come through the valley with a different kind of vision.
He no longer saw God as a system to master, but as a Presence to trust.

That's what integrity becomes when it's refined by fire:
a faith that limps, but doesn't let go.

So if you're standing in ashes—
If you're carrying questions that don't come with answers—
Take heart.

Because Job's story doesn't tell us how to avoid suffering.
It teaches us how to **stay with God through it**.

Not with perfection.
Not with platitudes.
But with the kind of honesty that heaven welcomes.

Because in the end, it wasn't Job's arguments that moved the heart of God.
It was his voice.

Round 4: Job – The Fight for Integrity

He kept talking.

And the Voice that thundered from the whirlwind… answered.

The Rabbi Speaks

Come closer.

We are standing on sacred ground now—not because everything has been fixed, but because something deeper has been revealed.

Job has seen the whirlwind.
He has felt the unanswerable weight of divine presence.
And now, covered in dust and trembling with awe, he says something extraordinary:

"Surely I spoke of things I did not understand,
things too wonderful for me to know."

This is not guilt. This is *yirah*—holy fear, reverence, the kind of awe that melts pride but preserves dignity. In Hebrew, the word Job uses for "wonderful" is often tied to **God's acts of redemption**. He is not repenting for lamenting—he is repenting for assuming that lament could ever contain the full mystery of God.

And then comes the line—one we must not overlook.

הֲרֹב עִם־שַׁדַּי יִסּוֹר
ha-rov im Shaddai yissor
"Shall the one wrestling with Shaddai still instruct Him?" (Job 40:2)

Do you hear it?

God calls Job a wrestler.

Not a blasphemer.
Not a doubter.
Not a disobedient man.
Page | 254

Round 4: Job – The Fight for Integrity

A *wrestler.*

And He does **not** rebuke him for it.

This echoes a much older name—Ya'akov, *Jacob*, the one who wrestled with God and came away limping but blessed. Job too walks away limping. But now he walks with something more than answers. He walks with God's favor.

This is not the theology most Western pews are used to.
In the East, however, this is how covenant works:
The righteous struggle *with* God, not *against* Him.
They cry out. They push back. They hold on.

And that kind of struggle is called *faith.*

Now, look at what happens next. Most eyes glaze over here—restoration, livestock, numbers. But the Hebrew writer has one final flourish. He lingers not on Job's wealth, but on his **daughters**.

"The first daughter he named Jemimah,
the second Keziah,
and the third Keren-Happuch."

Three names. Three poems in a culture where women were rarely even mentioned in genealogies.

Jemimah: "dove"—a symbol of peace after chaos.
Keziah: "cassia"—a spice of the temple, used in sacred anointing.
Keren-Happuch: "horn of eye-paint"—an image of beauty, adornment, restoration.

And then this:

Round 4: Job – The Fight for Integrity

"Nowhere in all the land were there found women as beautiful as Job's daughters…"

Do you see?
The story doesn't end with an argument. It ends with **beauty**.
With women being seen, named, and **given inheritance**—something unheard of in ancient times.

This is the quiet revolution of the Hebrew text.
God not only restores Job's fortune—He expands his vision.
From ashes to daughters.
From loss to legacy.
From lament to names written into eternity.

So sit with this:

God did not give Job an explanation.
He gave him a voice in the whirlwind, a name in the ashes, and daughters who would carry the light forward.

Not a reset.
A resurrection.

And it began the moment Job *stayed in the conversation*.

The Fighter Speaks

I didn't return to the world the same way I left it.
I carried the ashes with me.
Not as a badge of shame…
But as proof that I had been somewhere sacred.

You may look at me now—wealth restored, family returned, life rebuilt.
But I remember what it cost.

Round 4: Job – The Fight for Integrity

I remember the graves.
I remember the silence.
I remember the long nights asking questions I never got answers to.

But I also remember the moment His voice broke through the whirlwind.
I remember that He spoke.
And in that moment, everything shifted.

Not because I finally understood…
But because I finally *saw*.

I said, "My ears had heard of You, but now my eyes have seen You."
And once you've seen Him—not the idea of Him, not the doctrine, but *Him*—
you can never walk the same.

I thought the fight was about justice.
But maybe it was about presence.
Maybe it was about learning how to hold on when everything is trying to tear you loose.

I didn't get an explanation.
I got a voice.

I didn't get justice.
I got a presence.

And somehow… I can live with that.

Because if I can still feel Him—
Even in the ashes,
Even after the loss,
Even when I am not who I once was…

Then the fight was not in vain.

Round 4: Job – The Fight for Integrity

I didn't walk away victorious.
But I didn't walk away empty.

I walk with a limp.
I walk with a deeper kind of wisdom.
And I walk with names—names I never expected to write down:
Jemimah. Keziah. Keren-Happuch.

Peace. Holiness. Beauty.

My daughters. My future.
My inheritance after the storm.

The Corner Man Speaks (Final Section)

You think I only came to roar.

You hear My questions and think they're daggers—
but they're scaffolding, son.
They're reminders that you're still small,
but not forgotten.

I needed you to feel how vast I am.
But not to shrink you.
To steady you.

Because I am not just the Voice in the whirlwind.
I am the One who answers you there.

I asked, "Where were you?"
Not to shame you—
but to remind you that I've always been where you couldn't be.

I laid the foundation,
but I never left your side.

Round 4: Job – The Fight for Integrity

And now that your fists have fallen,
and your strength is spent,
I can draw near.

Because I don't want to crush you.

I want to hold you.

In This Corner: Job – The Fight for Integrity
He didn't swing his fists.

He opened his wounds.

And somehow, that was enough.

Job steps into the ring not with a roar, but with a groan. His wealth stripped, his body broken, his children buried—he raises no sword, makes no defense. He simply stays. That's the miracle of Job: not that he triumphed, but that he *remained*. He stayed in the conversation. He stayed in the ashes. He stayed with God.

His friends quoted doctrines; Job quoted pain.
His wife said, "Curse God and die"; Job said, "Though He slay me, yet will I hope in Him."
He questioned, accused, lamented—yes. But he *never walked away*.

And that, in the end, is what God calls righteous.

Not the ones who explained Him.
The one who *wrestled* Him.

He was called **blameless**, not flawless.
He was honored for his **integrity**, not his certainty.
Because in the Hebrew imagination, the righteous are not those who never weep, but those who **weep toward God**.

God doesn't silence Job's voice. He *answers* it. Not with explanations, but with presence.
Not with comfort, but with questions that reframe the universe.

And then—after the questions have settled and the whirlwind has passed—comes the restoration. Not as a reward for being right. But as the fruit of refusing to let go.

Round 4: Job – The Fight for Integrity

Job is given back more than he lost. But the deeper gift?
A voice that *saw* God, not just heard of Him.
A wisdom that grew from wounds.
A faith that limps, but keeps walking.

So when your own storm comes—when the loss is fresh and the sky is
silent—remember:
You don't need polished words.
You don't need perfect theology.
You need honesty. And integrity. And breath enough to say,
"I'm still here."

Because in this ring, victory doesn't look like understanding.
It looks like *endurance*.

Job didn't win the argument.
He won the blessing.

Because he stayed in the fight.

Round 5

The Fight for Belonging

Ruth 1:1-22 The Empty House

📖 *Ruth 1:1–22*

This subchapter frames the inciting moment of Ruth's journey — a descent into loss, displacement, and identity crisis. The house of Elimelek has collapsed, leaving Naomi and Ruth with nothing but a name, a memory, and a long walk home.

Ruth 1:1–22 (NIV)

In the days when the judges ruled, there was a famine in the land. So a man from Bethlehem in Judah, together with his wife and two sons, went to live for a while in the country of Moab. The man's name was Elimelek, his wife's name was Naomi, and the names of his two sons were Mahlon and Kilion. They were Ephrathites from Bethlehem, Judah. And they went to Moab and lived there.

Now Elimelek, Naomi's husband, died, and she was left with her two sons. They married Moabite women, one named Orpah and the other Ruth. After they had lived there about ten years, both Mahlon and Kilion also died, and Naomi was left without her two sons and her husband.

When Naomi heard in Moab that the Lord had come to the aid of his people by providing food for them, she and her daughters-in-law prepared to return home from there. With her two daughters-in-law she left the place where she had been living and set out on the road that would take them back to the land of Judah.

Then Naomi said to her two daughters-in-law, "Go back, each of you, to your mother's home. May the Lord show you kindness, as you have shown kindness to your dead husbands and to me. May the Lord grant that each of you will find rest in the home of another husband." Then she kissed them goodbye and they wept aloud and said to her, "We will go back with you to your people."

But Naomi said, "Return home, my daughters. Why would you come with me? Am I going to have any more sons, who could become your husbands? Return home, my daughters; I am too old to have another husband. Even if I thought there was still hope for me—even if I had a husband tonight and then gave birth to sons—would you wait until they grew up? Would you remain unmarried for them? No, my daughters. It is more bitter for me than for you, because the Lord's hand has turned against me!"

At this they wept aloud again. Then Orpah kissed her mother-in-law goodbye, but Ruth clung to her.

"Look," said Naomi, "your sister-in-law is going back to her people and her gods. Go back with her."

But Ruth replied, "Don't urge me to leave you or to turn back from you. Where you go I will go, and where you stay I will stay. Your people will be my people and your God my God. Where you die I will die, and there I will be buried. May the Lord deal with me, be it ever so severely, if even death separates you and me."

When Naomi realized that Ruth was determined to go with her, she stopped urging her.

So the two women went on until they came to Bethlehem. When they arrived in Bethlehem, the whole town was stirred because of them, and the women exclaimed, "Can this be Naomi?"

"Don't call me Naomi," she told them. "Call me Mara, because the Almighty has made my life very bitter. I went away full, but the Lord has brought me back empty. Why call me Naomi? The Lord has afflicted me; the Almighty has brought misfortune upon me."

So Naomi returned from Moab accompanied by Ruth the Moabite, her daughter-in-law, arriving in Bethlehem as the barley harvest was beginning.

The Preacher Speaks

Some stories in Scripture begin with fire — burning bushes, angelic visions, seas split in two.
But Ruth's story?
It begins with silence.
No miracles. No manifestations.
Just famine, funerals, and the quiet shuffle of feet leaving home.

It was "the days when the judges ruled," a time when everyone did what was right in their own eyes.
A time of disorientation, fragmentation, and wandering.
But this isn't a national crisis. Not yet.
It's a personal collapse.
One house. One woman. One name unraveling in a foreign land.

Naomi. Once pleasant. Now bitter.
She lost her husband, then her sons, then herself.
She doesn't curse God, but she doesn't defend Him either.
She just tells the truth as she feels it:
"The Lord's hand has turned against me."

Have you ever felt that?
Like maybe God didn't just *allow* your suffering — maybe He *assigned* it.
Like you're still in the story, but you're not sure if you're still the beloved.

And yet, in the middle of that bitter soil, something sacred takes root.
Not a voice from heaven. Not a pillar of cloud.
Just a whisper. A rumor.
"She heard that the Lord had come to the aid of His people…"

That's all.
Not a breakthrough — a breadcrumb.
And sometimes, that's how redemption begins.
Not with fireworks, but with famine and a flicker of hope.

So Naomi sets her face toward Bethlehem — the House of Bread —
not because she's full of faith, but because she's hungry enough to try.

And then there's Ruth.
A Moabite.
A descendant of Lot — the man Abraham once risked everything to
rescue.
Ruth comes from that lineage. That scandal. That side story in Genesis
that most of us skip.
But God doesn't skip it.
Because the God of Scripture weaves redemptive loops out of broken
beginnings.
He lets Ruth — the outsider, the other, the unwanted branch — cling
to Naomi, cling to covenant, and in doing so, cling to the God of
Abraham.

She doesn't know she's stepping into legacy.
She doesn't know she's walking toward Boaz, toward David, toward
Bethlehem's greater Son.
She only knows that bitterness won't get the last word if she has
anything to say about it.

And Naomi?
She doesn't come home with victory.
She comes home with *presence*.
She says, "Call me Mara."
She gives her grief a name — and lets it speak.

That's faith, too.
Not the kind that shouts in the sanctuary,

but the kind that limps back to Bethlehem
with a Moabite shadow and a broken name
and a wild, flickering hope that maybe God is still writing.

The Rabbi Speaks

Come, student.
Let us not walk past the silence too quickly.
This story opens not with fire, but with famine. Not with glory, but
with grief. And in Hebrew, grief is not an interruption — it is often the
very language God speaks.

The setting is Moab.
A land not just foreign, but infamous.
Its name — *Moav* (מוֹאָב) — means "from father," and its origin is not
hidden.
It was born in a cave, in the shame-shadowed escape of Lot and his
eldest daughter.
Moab is not just geography. It is memory. It is exile. It is the echo of
decisions made in fear.

And yet... *here* is where the seed of redemption begins.

The text tells us Ruth is from Moab, but it does not define her by it.
She does not remain what the past says she must be.
Instead, she speaks a vow — one of the clearest declarations of
covenant in all of Scripture:
"Your people will be my people, and your God my God."

These are not polite words.
They are *chesed* (חֶסֶד).
A word deeper than loyalty.
Chesed is covenantal love that acts with fierce devotion even when it
has no obligation to do so.

Round 5: Ruth — The Fight for Belonging

It is the love that clings even when it could let go.
And in Ruth, *chesed* takes on flesh.

But there is another word hidden in this first chapter — one that
repeats like a heartbeat: *shuv* (שׁוּב).
It means "to return."
Naomi uses it again and again.
Return to your people.
Return to your gods.
Return to Bethlehem.

But in Hebrew, *shuv* is never only physical. It is spiritual. It is
directional.
And when it deepens, it becomes *teshuvah* — the sacred act of
repentance, of turning the heart back to its true source.

Ruth's steps are not just steps toward Israel.
They are steps into identity, into transformation, into grafting.
She is not just walking beside Naomi — she is walking into the
covenant family.
Not by blood.
Not by law.
But by *chesed* and *shuv*.

This is the way of the Holy One.
To take the dust of Lot's shame and shape it into the legacy of David.
To begin redemption not in the palace, but in the silence of a bitter
woman and the loyalty of a Moabite daughter-in-law.

So do not despise the empty house.
Do not overlook the footnotes of genealogy.
Because hidden in these low places are the fingerprints of the Messiah.

The Fighter Speaks

I didn't grow up with this God.

Round 5: Ruth — The Fight for Belonging

I grew up with altars of stone and names I couldn't pronounce and gods that had eyes but didn't see.
In Moab, we learned survival, not hope.
Grief was something you buried quickly. Bitterness was something you wore quietly.
And women like me… we weren't supposed to follow stories like this.

But then I married into Naomi's house —
a house that once laughed, once prayed, once believed the famine would end.
And then it didn't.

The men died.
The music stopped.
And all that was left was dust, silence, and a mother-in-law who didn't know who she was anymore.

I could've left.
Everyone told me to.

Go back, they said.
Back to your people.
Back to your gods.
Back to the story written for girls like you.

But something in me refused to turn back.
Not because I understood everything — but because I knew *emptiness shouldn't travel alone.*

Naomi said she was going home.
Said she was bitter. Said she was done.
But I saw something in her — something still breathing, even beneath the grief.
She walked like someone who'd once believed in a God who keeps His word.

Round 5: Ruth — The Fight for Belonging

And I wanted that.
Even if it killed me.

So I opened my mouth and made a vow.

Where you go, I'll go.
Where you stay, I'll stay.
Your people… my people.
Your God… my God.

I didn't say it to be poetic.
I said it because I was already burning the bridges behind me.
I wasn't going back to Moab.
I wasn't going back to small gods with small names.

I was walking into a foreign land with nothing but loyalty in my fists.
Not faith — not yet.
But something like it.
Something called *chesed* — that stubborn kind of love that doesn't let go.

So when she said she came back empty, I stayed silent.
But in my chest, I thought:

Then what am I?

Because I was still standing.
Still holding the vow.
Still walking beside her.

And maybe I was a stranger.
Maybe I was a remnant of a family she'd rather forget.
But I was also the first sign that her house was not yet finished.
Not with walls.
Not with blood.
But with *covenant*.

Round 5: Ruth — The Fight for Belonging

I didn't come to find a name.
I came to carry one forward.

The Corner Man Speaks

You followed her.

When everything around you said "return,"
when the road grew dry and the names grew cold,
you walked forward — not with certainty, but with *something stronger*.

You gave up your gods, your country, your bloodline.
But I never asked you to become someone else.
I just asked you to be faithful with your yes.

You clung to a woman the world called bitter.
But I saw the beauty in your grip.
You held on to her like a remnant holds on to promise.
You didn't walk into Bethlehem to be seen —
you walked to stay close.
And that was enough.

They didn't notice you at first.
They saw Naomi and her shadow.
They heard the grief.
They missed the seed standing beside her.

But I didn't miss it.
I never miss a seed.

You stood in the doorway of a house that had forgotten its name.
And with nothing but loyalty in your voice,
you renamed it.

Round 5: Ruth — The Fight for Belonging

Not with a sermon.
Not with a miracle.
But with *presence*.

They said Naomi came back empty.
But I saw your vow, and I called it full.

Because what you carried — even if you couldn't see it —
was legacy.
Redemption.
The bloodline of the Shepherd-King.

You came from Moab, yes.
From Lot's ruin.
From history's footnote.
But I do my best work with broken branches.

And one day, they will speak your name not with suspicion,
but with *reverence*.

Ruth.
The outsider who became the matriarch.
The silence who became the story.
The one who held on — and refused to let go.

Ruth 2:1-23 Gleaning in a Foreign Field

📖 *Ruth 2:1–23*

- Ruth steps into the margins, gathering scraps
- She labors under stigma as a Moabite outsider
- Boaz notices her hesed (covenant loyalty)
- Quiet dignity begins to be honored

Ruth 2:1–23 (NIV)

Now Naomi had a relative on her husband's side, a man of standing from the clan of Elimelek, whose name was Boaz.

And Ruth the Moabite said to Naomi, "Let me go to the fields and pick up the leftover grain behind anyone in whose eyes I find favor." Naomi said to her, "Go ahead, my daughter."

So she went out, entered a field and began to glean behind the harvesters. As it turned out, she was working in a field belonging to Boaz, who was from the clan of Elimelek.

Just then Boaz arrived from Bethlehem and greeted the harvesters, "The Lord be with you!"
"The Lord bless you!" they answered.

Boaz asked the overseer of his harvesters, "Who does that young woman belong to?"

The overseer replied, "She is the Moabite who came back from Moab with Naomi. She said, 'Please let me glean and gather among the sheaves behind the harvesters.' She came into the field and has remained here from morning till now, except for a short rest in the shelter."

Round 5: Ruth — The Fight for Belonging

So Boaz said to Ruth, "My daughter, listen to me. Don't go and glean in another field and don't go away from here. Stay here with the women who work for me. Watch the field where the men are harvesting, and follow along after the women. I have told the men not to lay a hand on you. And whenever you are thirsty, go and get a drink from the water jars the men have filled."

At this, she bowed down with her face to the ground. She asked him, "Why have I found such favor in your eyes that you notice me—a foreigner?"

Boaz replied, "I've been told all about what you have done for your mother-in-law since the death of your husband—how you left your father and mother and your homeland and came to live with a people you did not know before.
May the Lord repay you for what you have done. May you be richly rewarded by the Lord, the God of Israel, under whose wings you have come to take refuge."

"May I continue to find favor in your eyes, my lord," she said. "You have put me at ease by speaking kindly to your servant—though I do not have the standing of one of your servants."

At mealtime Boaz said to her, "Come over here. Have some bread and dip it in the wine vinegar."
When she sat down with the harvesters, he offered her some roasted grain. She ate all she wanted and had some left over.

As she got up to glean, Boaz gave orders to his men, "Let her gather among the sheaves and don't reprimand her. Even pull out some stalks for her from the bundles and leave them for her to pick up, and don't rebuke her."

So Ruth gleaned in the field until evening. Then she threshed the barley she had gathered, and it amounted to about an ephah.

She carried it back to town, and her mother-in-law saw how much she had gathered. Ruth also brought out and gave her what she had left over after she had eaten enough.

Her mother-in-law asked her, "Where did you glean today? Where did you work? Blessed be the man who took notice of you!"

Then Ruth told her mother-in-law about the one at whose place she had been working.
"The name of the man I worked with today is Boaz," she said.

"The Lord bless him!" Naomi said to her daughter-in-law. "He has not stopped showing his kindness to the living and the dead." She added, "That man is our close relative; he is one of our guardian-redeemers."

Then Ruth the Moabite said, "He even said to me, 'Stay with my workers until they finish harvesting all my grain.'"

Naomi said to Ruth her daughter-in-law, "It will be good for you, my daughter, to go with the women who work for him, because in someone else's field you might be harmed."

So Ruth stayed close to the women of Boaz to glean until the barley and wheat harvests were finished. And she lived with her mother-in-law.

The Preacher Speaks

There are days when the miracle looks like a handful of grain.

Not fire from heaven. Not seas parting.
Just a woman with empty hands bending low to gather what others left behind.

Ruth doesn't wake up to destiny.
She wakes up to *need*.
She looks at Naomi, still hollowed out by loss, and says, "Let me go to

the fields…"
No fanfare. No vision. Just quiet resolve wrapped in daily obedience.

And Scripture adds a phrase that changes everything:
"As it turned out…"
As it turned out, she was gleaning in Boaz's field.

But nothing just *turns out* in the hands of God.

This is what favor often looks like:
A stranger in a strange field.
A silence that stretches between grief and hope.
A land that isn't hers, harvesting a story she doesn't yet know she's in.

Boaz notices her.
Not because she's beautiful — though she may be.
Not because she's impressive — though her courage is.
He notices her because she's faithful.
Because the way she cares for Naomi echoes the character of a God who never leaves the widowed or the poor behind.

And when she asks him, *"Why have I found such favor in your eyes, that you notice me — a foreigner?"*
She speaks for all of us.

Who among us hasn't stood in the field of grace, wondering why we were seen at all?

Boaz speaks blessing over her — not because she earned it, but because she revealed it.
Because her loyalty is *chesed* made visible.
Because her heart is already aligned with the God she barely knows.

And then he feeds her.

Round 5: Ruth — The Fight for Belonging

Bread.
Roasted grain.
Leftovers enough to bring home.

It's not a feast.
But it's enough.

Enough to remind her that hunger isn't her only inheritance.
That belonging isn't always earned — sometimes it's *noticed*.
Sometimes it finds you bent over in a field you don't deserve,
and says: "Stay close."

There's no wedding yet. No romance.
But there is provision.
There is presence.
There is the slow unfolding of a story that began with famine and is
now filling with favor.

And that is often how God writes:
Grain by grain.
Kindness by kindness.
Until the field becomes a doorway,
and the gleaner becomes the one who will carry the promise forward.

The Rabbi Speaks

Come closer, student. Let us enter the field not as farmers, but as
listeners. The soil here does not just grow grain — it grows mercy.

In Israel, the poor were not left to starve. The Torah commanded that
the corners of the field remain unharvested, the dropped sheaves left
untouched.
This practice is called **leket** (לֶקֶט) — gleaning — and it was more than
charity. It was dignity.
It said: *You may have little, but you are not forgotten.*

Round 5: Ruth — The Fight for Belonging

And so Ruth, the Moabite, enters this field not as a thief, but as one *invited by law*.
Yet even with that legal allowance, she walks with caution.
She asks permission.
She gleans from behind.
She knows the way the world looks at women like her.

And the text makes sure to remind us: she is still called *Ruth the Moabite*.

Why?

Because names matter.
Because the authors want us to feel the weight of her identity —
outsider, foreigner, descendant of Lot, daughter of exile.
She does not yet belong.
But she is learning to stay.

And then comes a phrase rare in the Hebrew scroll:

"Her chance chanced upon the field of Boaz."
That's how it reads.
Vayiker mikrehah chelek sadat Boaz (וַיִּקֶר מִקְרֶהָ חֶלְקַת שָׂדֶה בֹעַז)

A double echo of "chance."
A Hebraic way of saying, "There are no coincidences — but this feels like one."

In Jewish thought, divine providence often hides behind the veil of circumstance.
The rabbis call it *hester panim* — the hiding of God's face.
But just because the face is hidden, does not mean the hand is absent.

Boaz arrives. He greets his workers with a blessing — *"The Lord be with you."*
A small phrase, but it tells us everything.
He is not just a landowner. He is a man shaped by reverence.

Round 5: Ruth — The Fight for Belonging

And when he sees Ruth, he asks, *"To whom does she belong?"*
A loaded question in a patriarchal world.
But the answer he receives is not possession — it is reputation.
"She is the Moabite who came with Naomi."

Boaz listens.
He honors what he hears.
And then he speaks to Ruth not as a servant, not as a stranger, but as a daughter.
He says: *"You have come under the wings of the God of Israel."*

In Hebrew, the word is *kanaf* (כָּנָף) — wing, corner, covering.
It's the same word used for the *tzitzit*, the corner fringes of a prayer shawl.
It is a symbol of refuge, of covenant, of nearness.

He blesses her — not because she has proven herself, but because she has chosen to draw close.

And here, dear student, the Torah and the heart of God align.
The law made space for Ruth to glean.
But love made space for her to belong.

The Fighter Speaks

The field was not mine.
The land was not mine.
Even the air here felt borrowed.

But I stepped into it anyway.
Because hunger doesn't wait for permission.

I asked Naomi if I could go — not because I needed her blessing,
but because I needed her to know I hadn't given up.

I walked out with no map.
No promise.
Just the hope that someone might leave behind enough for us to make it one more day.

I didn't know his name.
Didn't know the rules.
I only knew how to keep my head down and my hands moving.

Gleaning isn't glorious.
It's slow, dirty work.
You gather what's left — the missed stalks, the broken stems, the pieces no one thought were worth keeping.

That's how I felt too, if I'm honest.
Missed.
Broken.
Left behind.

But then… he saw me.
Boaz.

He didn't speak to me like I was a burden.
He didn't warn me to stay in my place.
He called me daughter.

And in that moment, something shifted.

He told me to stay in his field.
To glean safely.
To drink water drawn by men I didn't even know.

And I couldn't help but ask: *Why?*

Why would someone like you notice someone like me?

Round 5: Ruth — The Fight for Belonging

I'm not from here.
I don't belong.
My story began in Moab — in shadows, in shame, in silence.

But Boaz said he'd *heard*.
He knew what I'd done for Naomi.
How I'd left everything behind and stepped into a life I didn't understand.

He said the God of Israel would reward me —
that I had come to take refuge under His wings.

I didn't know that's what I was doing.

I only knew I couldn't go back.

He gave me bread.
Roasted grain.
More than I needed.
More than I expected.

I ate until I was full.
Then I saved the rest for Naomi.

Because that's what you do when you know what it's like to be empty.

I walked home with arms full and heart trembling.
She asked me where I'd been.
I told her his name.

Boaz.

She said he was a redeemer.

I didn't know what that meant.
Not yet.
But I knew I'd found a field I didn't want to leave.

Round 5: Ruth — The Fight for Belonging

A name I wanted to trust.
A God I was just beginning to believe might be watching all along.

The Corner Man Speaks

I saw you step into that field.

Not with pride, but with purpose.
Not with answers, but with empty hands and a heart still aching.
You didn't demand favor.
You gathered it — grain by grain, grace by grace.

And I called it holy.

You didn't know the land.
Didn't know the language.
Didn't know the name Boaz would carry in your story.
But still, you walked.

Still, you gleaned.

You bent low where others walked tall.
You asked for nothing but space in the corner.
And I watched you take what little was left and turn it into enough.

I saw the way you looked at Naomi —
not as a burden, but as a blessing.
You carried her grief like your own.
You fed her before you fed yourself.
And when the field gave you bread,
you made it a table.

And Boaz?
He wasn't just kindness.
He was a mirror.

Round 5: Ruth — The Fight for Belonging

He spoke the words I had always spoken over you:
You are not forgotten. You are not alone. You are not too far gone.

Under his wing, you found shelter.
But under Mine, you found story.

You thought you were picking up scraps.
But you were gathering legacy.
You thought you were surviving.
But you were stepping into prophecy.

Because this field —
this moment —
this handful of grain —
was always more than it seemed.

One day, your name will be remembered not for where you came from,
but for what you carried forward.

You, Ruth —
foreign and faithful,
widowed and willing —
will become the womb through which kings rise.

And every woman who wonders if she matters,
every outsider who thinks they don't belong,
every soul who stoops just to make it to tomorrow —
will hear your story
and remember:

I see them too.

Ruth 3:1-18 The Threshing Floor Risk

📖 *Ruth 3:1–18*

- Naomi urges Ruth to risk again
- A Moabite woman, under cover of night, asks for redemption
- The shadow of Lot's daughters lingers—but this is no manipulation
- Ruth's courage is covenantal, not conniving

Ruth 3:1–18 (NIV)

One day Ruth's mother-in-law Naomi said to her, "My daughter, I must find a home for you, where you will be well provided for.
Now Boaz, with whose women you have worked, is a relative of ours. Tonight he will be winnowing barley on the threshing floor.
Wash, put on perfume, and get dressed in your best clothes. Then go down to the threshing floor, but don't let him know you are there until he has finished eating and drinking.
When he lies down, note the place where he is lying. Then go and uncover his feet and lie down. He will tell you what to do."

"I will do whatever you say," Ruth answered.
So she went down to the threshing floor and did everything her mother-in-law told her to do.

When Boaz had finished eating and drinking and was in good spirits, he went over to lie down at the far end of the grain pile. Ruth approached quietly, uncovered his feet and lay down.

In the middle of the night something startled the man; he turned—and there was a woman lying at his feet!

"Who are you?" he asked.

"I am your servant Ruth," she said. "Spread the corner of your garment over me, since you are a guardian-redeemer of our family."

"The Lord bless you, my daughter," he replied. "This kindness is greater than that which you showed earlier: You have not run after the younger men, whether rich or poor.
And now, my daughter, don't be afraid. I will do for you all you ask. All the people of my town know that you are a woman of noble character.
Although it is true that I am a guardian-redeemer of our family, there is another who is more closely related than I.
Stay here for the night, and in the morning if he wants to do his duty as your guardian-redeemer, good; let him redeem you.
But if he is not willing, as surely as the Lord lives I will do it. Lie here until morning."

So she lay at his feet until morning, but got up before anyone could be recognized; and he said, "No one must know that a woman came to the threshing floor."

He also said, "Bring me the shawl you are wearing and hold it out." When she did so, he poured into it six measures of barley and placed the bundle on her. Then he went back to town.

When Ruth came to her mother-in-law, Naomi asked, "How did it go, my daughter?"

Then she told her everything Boaz had done for her and added, "He gave me these six measures of barley, saying, 'Don't go back to your mother-in-law empty-handed.'"

Then Naomi said, "Wait, my daughter, until you find out what happens. For the man will not rest until the matter is settled today."

Round 5: Ruth — The Fight for Belonging

The Preacher Speaks

There are moments in Scripture that feel like a held breath.

This is one of them.

Naomi has a plan. Not a manipulative one — a desperate one.
She's seen the favor. She's seen the field.
Now she's wondering if maybe the hand of God isn't just feeding them
— maybe it's *redeeming* them.

So she sends Ruth to the threshing floor.
Not to seduce.
To *ask*.

Wash. Anoint. Dress.
Wait until the feasting is done.
Find him where he rests, uncover his feet, and lie down.

No words at first.
Just presence.
Just vulnerability.

And when Boaz wakes — startled, unsure — Ruth speaks.

Not a plea. Not a demand.
A request wrapped in covenant language:
"Spread the corner of your garment over me."

She's not asking for protection.
She's asking for *belonging*.

She's invoking the symbol of marriage, of redemption, of covenant
covering — the same word Boaz used earlier when he said she had
come under the wings of God.

Now she's asking Boaz to embody the very grace he blessed her with.

Round 5: Ruth — The Fight for Belonging

This is what boldness looks like in the kingdom:
Not grabbing power.
But naming hope.
Risking rejection.
Laying yourself down where only the brave lie.

And Boaz — to his credit — doesn't run.
He doesn't take advantage.
He doesn't shame her.

He speaks *blessing.*
He calls her kindness greater now than it was before.
He promises to act — not with hesitation, but with *haste.*
And before she leaves, he fills her shawl with grain — six measures,
heavy with meaning — and sends her back to Naomi.

Empty-handed no more.

Ruth goes home not with a ring, but with a promise.
Not with certainty, but with hope that's starting to take shape.

Naomi sees the grain, hears the words, and smiles with the wisdom of
someone who knows how redemption moves:
"The man will not rest until the matter is settled today."

And neither will God.

The Rabbi Speaks

Ruth – Subchapter 3: The Threshing Floor

Come, student.
Let us approach the threshing floor gently.
It is not only a place of grain. It is a place of *testing.*

In Hebrew thought, the threshing floor is where the harvest is purified
—

where the kernel is separated from the husk,
where the wind helps reveal what is true.

So when Naomi sends Ruth here, it is not to chase romance —
it is to step into *risk and revelation.*

Naomi says, *"Wash, anoint, dress."*
This is not seduction.
This is preparation.

In Hebrew, these words mirror the ancient rituals of **consecration.**
A bride before a covenant.
A priest before service.
One preparing to enter holy space.

And Ruth listens.

She goes quietly.
She lies at Boaz's feet — not at his side, not in his bed —
and waits.

Then comes the moment that turns the story:
She says,
"Spread your garment over me, for you are a go'el."
A **go'el** (גֹּאֵל) — a kinsman-redeemer.

But the word she uses for garment is **kanaf** (כָּנָף).
We've seen it before.

Kanaf means wing.
It is the edge of a garment, yes — but also the image of God's
covering.
Like a mother bird gathering her young beneath her feathers.
Like the corners of a tallit, the prayer shawl that wraps a life in
covenant.

Round 5: Ruth — The Fight for Belonging

She is not just asking Boaz for marriage.
She is asking him to do what God does:
To cover.
To redeem.
To bring what was lost back into belonging.

This is not a Moabite request.
This is Israelite *faith* spoken in the language of hesed.

And Boaz hears it.
He calls her a woman of **chayil** (חַיִל) — noble character, strength, valor.
The same word used for warriors.
The same word used for the Proverbs 31 woman.

Ruth is no longer just the gleaner.
She is the vessel of legacy.

But Boaz does not presume.
He says: *There is one closer than I. If he redeems, good. If not, I will.*

Here we learn something else about covenant:
It honors the path, even when it costs us time.

Ruth lies at his feet until morning.
She leaves before the sun names her.
And in her arms she carries **six measures** of barley.

The sages say the number six represents incompletion —
the days before Sabbath.
The world waiting for rest.
The promise not yet fulfilled, but close.

Boaz sends her back not with finality,
but with a message wrapped in grain:
"Wait. Redemption is moving."

The Fighter Speaks

I lay down at his feet.
Not to beg.
Not to seduce.
But to be seen.

I had gleaned the corners of his field.
Now I was asking…
Is there a corner in *you*
where I could belong?

Naomi said wash.
Anoint.
Dress.
Go.

And I did — but it wasn't romance.
It was courage.
It was the soft kind, the kind that trembles while it walks.
The kind you carry when your only weapon is *hope*.

I waited for him to fall asleep.
Waited for the feast to settle, for the day to be done.
Then I stepped into the silence, uncovered his feet, and laid down.

And I waited.

My heartbeat was louder than the night.

When he stirred, I didn't know what he'd say.
Would he curse me? Send me away? Pretend he didn't know my name?

But he asked, "Who are you?"
And I answered with everything I had:
"I am Ruth.

Cover me.
You are a redeemer."

I wasn't just asking for a marriage.
I was asking for a future.
For a home.
For the right to no longer be the outsider in every room.

He could've turned away.
Instead, he spoke *blessing*.
He called me kind.
He said I was seen.
And I believed him.

He told me to stay until morning.
So I did.
Not as a servant.
Not as a scandal.
But as a woman waiting on the will of God to move.

And in the gray of dawn,
he filled my shawl with grain.
Six measures.
More than I could carry, but not enough to finish the story.

He gave me what he could,
and he gave it with dignity.

I walked back to Naomi heavy.
Not with shame — with *significance*.
She looked at the bundle.
Looked at my eyes.
And whispered,
"He won't rest until this is done."

And I believed her too.

Round 5: Ruth — The Fight for Belonging

I don't know what today holds.
But I know this:

I laid down in risk,
and I rose up remembered.

The Corner Man Speaks

You lay down in the dark.

No music.
No crowds.
No voice from heaven to tell you how this ends.

Just the sound of your own breath
and the weight of hope that was almost too heavy to carry.

You uncovered his feet.
But what you really uncovered… was *trust*.

You gave him no demands.
Only your name.
Only your heart.
Only the quiet courage to say,
"Cover me."

I was there.

I saw your fingers shake as you reached for his garment.
I saw your eyes scan the shadows, wondering if you had made a mistake.

But you didn't.

You stepped into a sacred risk —
the kind that turns strangers into family
and ashes into legacy.

Round 5: Ruth — The Fight for Belonging

You didn't come to steal something that wasn't yours.
You came to ask if you could belong.
And I called that holy.

Because I made you for more than gleaning behind others.
I made you to carry redemption through your body, through your
bloodline, through your *yes*.

And Boaz?
He didn't just see a woman at his feet.
He saw a future unfolding before him.

He saw what I see:
A Moabite with the heart of Israel.
A widow with the strength of warriors.
A daughter who dared to believe that someone might not just feed her,
but *fight for her*.

When he filled your shawl with barley,
he didn't just give you grain.
He gave you *assurance*.

The promise is not finished yet —
but it is *moving*.

You're not empty anymore.

You are not waiting alone.

You are wrapped in more than a shawl.
You are wrapped in My story.

And I never leave stories unfinished.

Ruth 4:1-12 At the City Gate

📖 *Ruth 4:1–12*

- The redemption is publicly sealed—not stolen in secrecy
- The closest redeemer backs out; Boaz steps in
- A once-forgotten woman is brought into the heart of Israel
- Her story now echoes Abraham's faith, not Lot's hesitation

Ruth 4:1–12 (NIV)

Boaz went up to the town gate and sat down there just as the guardian-redeemer he had mentioned came along.

Boaz said, "Come over here, my friend, and sit down." So he went over and sat down.

Boaz took ten of the elders of the town and said, "Sit here," and they did so.

Then he said to the guardian-redeemer, "Naomi, who has come back from Moab, is selling the piece of land that belonged to our relative Elimelek.

I thought I should bring the matter to your attention and suggest that you buy it in the presence of these seated here and in the presence of the elders of my people.

If you will redeem it, do so. But if you will not, tell me, so I will know. For no one has the right to do it except you, and I am next in line."

"I will redeem it," he said.

Then Boaz said, "On the day you buy the land from Naomi, you also acquire Ruth the Moabite, the dead man's widow, in order to maintain the name of the dead with his property."

At this, the guardian-redeemer said, "Then I cannot redeem it because I might endanger my own estate. You redeem it yourself. I cannot do it."

Round 5: Ruth — The Fight for Belonging

(Now in earlier times in Israel, for the redemption and transfer of property to become final, one party took off his sandal and gave it to the other. This was the method of legalizing transactions in Israel.)
So the guardian-redeemer said to Boaz, "Buy it yourself." And he removed his sandal.

Then Boaz announced to the elders and all the people,
"Today you are witnesses that I have bought from Naomi all the property of Elimelek, Kilion and Mahlon.
I have also acquired Ruth the Moabite, Mahlon's widow, as my wife, in order to maintain the name of the dead with his property,
so that his name will not disappear from among his family or from his hometown.
Today you are witnesses!"

Then the elders and all the people at the gate said,
"We are witnesses.
May the Lord make the woman who is coming into your home like Rachel and Leah,
who together built up the family of Israel.
May you have standing in Ephrathah and be famous in Bethlehem.
Through the offspring the Lord gives you by this young woman,
may your family be like that of Perez, whom Tamar bore to Judah."

The Preacher Speaks

There are places in Scripture where heaven whispers.
And then there are places where it *shouts*.

This is one of those places.

Boaz walks to the gate — not as a dreamer, not as a hopeful man with a heart full of barley and promises — but as a redeemer ready to *act*.

The gate isn't just a location.
It's the courtroom.

Round 5: Ruth — The Fight for Belonging

It's where legacy is written down in the presence of elders and strangers alike.
It's where private faith becomes public covenant.

He sits. He calls witnesses.
And he brings the unnamed relative into the open.

"Naomi has land," Boaz says. "Will you redeem it?"

And the man says yes — because redemption sounds easy until it costs you something.
But Boaz isn't finished.

He adds what the law *requires* but the man had not considered:
"With the land comes Ruth. The Moabite. The widow. The name of the dead must live on."

And suddenly, redemption isn't just property.
It's *people*.
It's inheritance.
It's reputation.
It's bloodline.

And that's when the man steps back.
"I cannot do it," he says.
"It would endanger my estate."

Translation:
It's too messy.
Too costly.
Too complicated.

And Boaz?
He doesn't hesitate.

Round 5: Ruth — The Fight for Belonging

He takes the sandal — the symbol of legal transfer —
and says in front of God and everyone:
"I will do it."

This isn't romance anymore.
This is redemption — chosen, claimed, sealed.

He names the land.
He names the line.
And he names Ruth — not as a foreigner, not as baggage, but as *bride*.

He says:
"I have acquired Ruth the Moabite as my wife... so that the name of the dead will not disappear."

That's covenant, friends.
That's the gospel in seed form.

And the people — oh, the people at the gate —
they rise with blessing on their lips:
"May she be like Rachel and Leah."
"May your name be known."
"May your family be like that of Perez..."

They don't curse her past.
They *bless her future.*

A Moabite woman once written off
is now written into the family of Israel —
and not just as a side note, but as the one who will carry kings in her womb.

Because God doesn't just redeem what's broken.
He *honors* it.
He *names* it.

Round 5: Ruth — The Fight for Belonging

He lifts it up in front of the elders and says:
"This is My story now."

The Rabbi Speaks

Come, student. Let us sit at the gate.

Not to spectate — but to witness.

This gate is not merely an entry point. In ancient Israel, the gate was the place of *justice*.
It is where elders sat, disputes were settled, and names were remembered or forgotten.

Boaz goes there early.
Not to delay.
Not to manipulate.
But to bring the matter into the light — where truth belongs.

Now hear his words again:
"Naomi is selling the land…"

This is the language of inheritance, of continuity, of *shalom*.
But it is incomplete.
Land without people is not legacy.
That is why Boaz adds:
"You must also acquire Ruth."

And here we must pause.

Because Ruth is not merely a widow.
She is a **Moabite** — and in Torah memory, Moab is exile, shame, and broken covenant.
Deuteronomy 23:3 forbids Moabites from entering the assembly for ten generations.

And yet…

Round 5: Ruth — The Fight for Belonging

Here she stands —
at the threshold of Israel's story,
at the intersection of hesed and halakhah.

Because the spirit of Torah is not exclusion —
it is **transformation**.

Boaz is not breaking the law.
He is fulfilling its *deepest purpose* —
to restore the name of the dead,
to protect the vulnerable,
to embody the kindness of the God who said,
"You shall not oppress the stranger, for you were strangers in Egypt."

And what of the sandal?

This ancient custom — removing one's sandal and handing it over —
is a visible sign of relinquishing redemption rights.
To give your sandal is to say:
"I step aside. I will not walk this path."

And Boaz?
He picks up the sandal like a mantle.
He does not just marry Ruth —
he takes on the *name* of Mahlon, her deceased husband,
so that the name would not be lost from among the living.

This is called **yibbum** — levirate marriage.
But here, it is more than obligation.
It is **covenantal love** made public.

And the people?

Ah, the people speak blessing.
They invoke **Rachel and Leah** — the mothers of Israel, the ones who
birthed tribes out of barrenness and rivalry.

Round 5: Ruth — The Fight for Belonging

They invoke **Perez**, the son of Tamar — another woman who fought for her place in the line.

Do you see, student?

Israel's story has always made room for those who fought to belong.
Always honored the women who risked shame for the sake of legacy.

And now Ruth stands among them —
no longer a foreigner,
but a *founder*.

Not just written into the scroll.
Woven into the seed of kings.

The Fighter Speaks

I wasn't there.

I didn't sit at the gate.
I didn't stand before elders.
I didn't speak my case.

But I was the reason the scroll was opened.
I was the question they had to answer.
I was the name behind the silence.

I waited on the other side — like I always have.
Like every woman who's ever prayed behind a wall.
Like every outsider whose future was being decided by voices that didn't know her pain.

But Boaz knew.

He didn't flinch when the cost came due.
He didn't rename me to make me more acceptable.
He didn't ask if I'd done enough to earn it.

Round 5: Ruth — The Fight for Belonging

He just stood up… and said **yes.**

Not to convenience.
To *covenant.*

He claimed me in front of everyone.
Not as a charity case.
Not as a tolerated stranger.
But as *his bride* —
a living link in a broken line he chose to restore.

The other man said,
"It's too risky."
And he was right.

I carry blood from Moab,
history from Lot,
the ache of graves in foreign soil.

But Boaz said,
"I'll carry it too."

And when he picked up the sandal,
he wasn't just closing a deal.
He was stepping into my story —
feet first, heart open.

I didn't hear the elders bless me.
But I felt it in my bones.

Rachel.
Leah.
Tamar.

Women who bore weight heavier than wombs —
who fought through silence and shame to bring forth legacy.

Round 5: Ruth — The Fight for Belonging

I'm one of them now.

Not because I proved myself.
But because I stayed.

I stayed loyal.
I stayed faithful.
I stayed when everything told me to go.

And that's what changed the story.

So no, I wasn't at the gate.

But my name passed through it —
not as a foreigner,
but as family.

The Corner Man Speaks

I watched you wait.

Not with impatience,
but with the quiet strength of someone who's handed her story to heaven
and said,
"Do what You will."

You didn't argue.
You didn't force your way into the conversation.
You let the truth speak for itself.

And I made sure it did.

While you stood unseen,
I stirred a man to stand on your behalf.
Not with poetry, but with promise.
Not in secret, but *in the open*.

Round 5: Ruth — The Fight for Belonging

Because redemption must be *witnessed*.

So I brought the elders.
I brought the scroll.
I brought the sandal.
And I made sure your name — the one they used to whisper with suspicion —
was now spoken with *blessing*.

I heard the man who said you were too risky.
Too foreign.
Too complicated.

And I let him walk away.

Because only one could carry the weight of this calling.
Only one could step into your story
and not be afraid of your fire.

Boaz said yes.
And in his yes, I wrote *Mine*.

You see, Ruth...
I was never just giving you provision.
I was preparing you for *promise*.

You thought you were gathering barley.
But I was gathering you.

You thought you were surviving.
But I was planting kings in your footsteps.

Now the gate has spoken.
And it did not echo with shame.
It rang with *inheritance*.

You belong.

Round 5: Ruth — The Fight for Belonging

Not just to Boaz.
Not just to Naomi.
Not just to Israel.

You belong to the line I've been weaving since before the world began.

And when generations whisper of kings and covenants,
when scrolls are opened and names are traced...

they will find *you* there.

Ruth 5:13-22 The Line of Kings

Ruth 4:13–22

- Ruth gives birth to Obed
- Naomi's sorrow is reversed
- The genealogy closes the loop: from Lot's cave to David's throne
- The outsider has become the mother of legacy

Ruth 4:13–22 (NIV)

So Boaz took Ruth and she became his wife.
When he made love to her, the Lord enabled her to conceive, and she gave birth to a son.
The women said to Naomi:
"Praise be to the Lord, who this day has not left you without a guardian-redeemer.
May he become famous throughout Israel!
He will renew your life and sustain you in your old age.
For your daughter-in-law, who loves you and who is better to you than seven sons, has given him birth."

Then Naomi took the child in her arms and cared for him.
The women living there said,
"Naomi has a son!"
And they named him Obed.
He was the father of Jesse, the father of David.

This, then, is the family line of Perez:

Perez was the father of Hezron,
Hezron the father of Ram,
Ram the father of Amminadab,
Amminadab the father of Nahshon,

Round 5: Ruth — The Fight for Belonging

Nahshon the father of Salmon,
Salmon the father of Boaz,
Boaz the father of Obed,
Obed the father of Jesse,
and Jesse the father of David.

The Preacher Speaks

This is how it ends — not with thunder or triumph,
but with a baby's breath and an old woman's arms full of promise.

Naomi, the one who said, "Call me Mara,"
now cradles new life against her chest.

She left Bethlehem in famine.
She returned in grief.
But here, at the end of the story, she is called *mother* once more.
Not because her own womb has opened again,
but because God has opened the future.

The women gather, not to mourn, but to rejoice.
They speak a blessing — not over Ruth, this time,
but over Naomi.

"Praise be to the Lord," they say,
"who has not left you without a redeemer."
They call Ruth better than seven sons —
and in that moment, the culture shifts.
A Moabite daughter-in-law becomes the model of covenant loyalty.

And then comes the name.

Obed.

It means "servant."
A name rooted in humility, in worship, in the steady work of the land.

Round 5: Ruth — The Fight for Belonging

It is not Ruth or Boaz who name him.
It is the community.
Because in Israel, a child belongs not just to a household,
but to a people.

And Obed's line — oh, his line —
will reach further than anyone could have imagined.

Obed becomes the father of Jesse.
Jesse, the father of David.

Yes, that David.
The boy with the sling.
The poet of psalms.
The man after God's own heart.

And there, tucked quietly behind the crown,
is the story of a woman who came from Moab,
who gleaned in fields she did not plant,
and who laid down at the feet of a redeemer with nothing but hope in
her hands.

She is not forgotten.
She is *foundational.*

Her kindness became legacy.
Her risk became royalty.
Her faith became a seed in the line that would one day birth a greater
King still.

Ruth's story ends with names.
But for those who can read between the lines,
it also ends with *echoes* —
echoes of another Redeemer,
who will come quietly, like a child,
and carry the same kind of love.

The kind that lifts the outsider.
That rewrites the ending.
That turns emptiness into a lineage of glory.

The Rabbi Speaks

Come close, student.

Let us unroll the scroll,
and trace the names not as footnotes…
but as **footsteps**.

Perez (פֶּרֶץ) — "the breach," the one who broke through.
Hezron.
Ram.
Amminadab.
Nahshon.
Salmon.
Boaz (בֹּעַז) — "in him is strength."
Obed (עֹבֵד) — "servant, worshiper."
Jesse (יִשַׁי) — "gift."
David (דָּוִד) — "beloved."

Do not rush past them.
Each name is a doorway.
Each name is a stone in the path of *ge'ulah* (גְּאֻלָּה) — **redemption**.

You may think this is the end of Ruth's story.
But in the Hebrew way of telling,
an ending is often the *beginning of fulfillment*.

And Ruth —
this **Moaviyah** (מוֹאָבִיָּה), this woman of Moab —
is now written into the very **toledot** (תּוֹלְדוֹת) — the *generations* —
that will give birth to kings.

Round 5: Ruth — The Fight for Belonging

But look again, not just at the men.
See the women between the lines.

Tamar — who risked shame for righteousness.
Ruth — who clung to hesed when she had nothing else.
And one day: **Mary** — *Miryam* (מִרְיָם) — who will say yes to the impossible.

This scroll ends with **Obed**.
But the rabbis say his name echoes forward.
Obed — the servant.
David — the beloved servant.
And from their line:
a greater Servant still…

One who will bear the brokenness of the world.
One who will fulfill **chesed** (חֶסֶד) — not just covenantal kindness,
but **costly loyalty, unwavering love, mercy that moves**.

Do you see?

Ruth's act at the threshing floor wasn't just bold —
it was **prophetic**.

When she asked Boaz to spread his *kanaf* (כָּנָף) —
his wing, his garment — over her,
she was echoing the cry of Israel:
"Hide me in the shadow of Your wings" (Psalm 17:8).

And God answered.
Not just through Boaz.
Through *Messiah*.

Because in the end, Ruth didn't just marry into a good family.
She was grafted into *the holy lineage of hope*.

Her womb carried wheat.
Her name carried a kingdom.

So do not read this scroll only with your eyes.
Read it with your heart.
And listen for the whisper of legacy in every name.

The Fighter Speaks

He placed the child in Naomi's arms.

And in that moment,
I knew the fight was over.

Not because the world changed.
But because *we had*.

Naomi wept — not bitter this time.
She wept like someone whose sorrow had been seen,
measured,
answered.

The women gathered and said,
"Naomi has a son."
They didn't say my name.
But I didn't need them to.

I was never in this for recognition.

I was in this for *redemption*.

And I got it.

Not just in barley.
Not just in a bridegroom.
But in this breath-wrapped-in-bloodline
that would one day shake the ground of kings.

Round 5: Ruth — The Fight for Belonging

His name is Obed.
Servant.

Because that's what this whole story has been.
Serving each other.
Serving hope.
Serving a God who never stopped writing us in.

You want to know how it ends?

It ends with a name —
and a line of names after it.

David.
The shepherd.
The psalmist.
The king.

And long after him,
when hope seemed buried again under silence and empire,
another baby would cry in Bethlehem.

Another Servant.
Another Redeemer.

And I believe —
somewhere in the mystery of heaven —
when His lineage was whispered into existence,
my name echoed in the chambers of God's heart.

Ruth.
The Moabite.
The widow.
The fighter.
The mother of kings.

Round 5: Ruth — The Fight for Belonging

I was never meant to be the center of the story.

I was just meant to *say yes*
when love came for me.

The Corner Man Speaks

You thought it was about survival.

Food.
Shelter.
A place to belong.

But I was never just feeding you.
I was *folding you in.*

From the first step out of Moab,
I was shaping your story for more than healing.

I was writing *history* through you.

You gleaned in fields you didn't plant.
You laid down in vulnerability and hope.
You followed kindness into covenant.

And I watched every moment.

I saw the way you didn't flinch when they whispered "Moabite."
I saw the courage it took to cling to Naomi when bitterness was easier.
I saw the risk in your request —
not for riches,
but for *covering.*

And now, you hold a child.
But what you really hold is the future.

Because through your body,
I brought a line of kings.

Round 5: Ruth — The Fight for Belonging

And one day,
through that line,
I will walk the earth Myself.

You are not the end of the story.
You are the root.

And when My Son is born in Bethlehem —
when shepherds come running and stars stand still —
heaven will remember that it started
with a widow in a foreign land
who believed love could still find her.

You never saw the crown.
But you carried it.

You never sat on the throne.
But you birthed it.

And Ruth —
they called you "outsider."
I call you *mine*.

In This Corner: Ruth – Round 5

You didn't think this would be your fight.
You thought you were just trying to survive.
Trying to make it through the grief.
Trying to carry someone else's loss while you buried your own.
You thought redemption was for *other* people — the clean ones, the ones with a name that didn't come with a backstory.

But you kept showing up.

You left the past behind.
You walked into fields that didn't belong to you.
You laid down at the feet of mercy, not because you were sure,
but because you were *willing*.

And heaven saw it.

Ruth didn't get to skip the silence.
She didn't get a shortcut to blessing.
She got famine.
She got stares.
She got called "Moabite" more times than she got called by name.

But she *stayed in the fight*.

And that's what changed everything.

Because while she was gathering barley,
God was gathering *kings* inside her future.
While she was grieving in shadows,
God was preparing a place for her name on royal scrolls.

And that same God —
the One who writes widows into bloodlines

Round 5: Ruth — The Fight for Belonging

and calls the barren "blessed" —
He's still writing today.

Your story isn't over.
You don't have to have it figured out.
You just have to stay in the ring.

Ruth didn't see the crown,
but she carried it.
And so do you.

So don't count yourself out.
Don't let your past define your prophecy.
And don't forget:

Some of the fiercest fighters in Scripture
never threw a punch.
They just stayed.

Round 6

The Fight to Wake the People

Judges 4:1-10 The Fight to Rise

Judges 4:1-10

- Israel once again falls into idolatry
- Deborah is introduced—not just as a prophetess, but as one who renders justice "under the Palm of Deborah"
- Her position is public, maternal, and Spirit-filled
- She does not seek power—she bears it with humility and clarity
- Deborah calls Barak to action
- God has already given victory—yet Barak wavers
- "If you go with me, I'll go," he says. A cry of fear wrapped in dependence
- Deborah agrees—but warns that the honor will go to a woman
- The theme of reluctant men and bold women rises again

Judges 4:1–10 (NIV)

Again the Israelites did evil in the eyes of the Lord, now that Ehud was dead.

So the Lord sold them into the hands of Jabin king of Canaan, who reigned in Hazor.

Sisera, the commander of his army, was based in Harosheth Haggoyim. Because he had nine hundred chariots fitted with iron and had cruelly oppressed the Israelites for twenty years, they cried to the Lord for help.

Now Deborah, a prophet, the wife of Lappidoth, was leading Israel at that time.

She held court under the Palm of Deborah between Ramah and Bethel in the hill country of Ephraim,

and the Israelites went up to her to have their disputes decided.

She sent for Barak son of Abinoam from Kedesh in Naphtali and said to him,
"The Lord, the God of Israel, commands you:
'Go, take with you ten thousand men of Naphtali and Zebulun and lead them up to Mount Tabor.
I will lead Sisera, the commander of Jabin's army, with his chariots and his troops to the Kishon River and give him into your hands.'"

Barak said to her,
"If you go with me, I will go; but if you don't go with me, I won't go."

"Certainly I will go with you," said Deborah.
"But because of the course you are taking, the honor will not be yours, for the Lord will deliver Sisera into the hands of a woman."
So Deborah went with Barak to Kedesh.

There Barak summoned Zebulun and Naphtali,
and ten thousand men went up under his command.
Deborah also went up with him.

The Preacher Speaks

You can almost hear the silence.

It had been twenty years since Israel had hope.
Twenty years of fear.
Twenty years of iron chariots grinding the ground underfoot.
And in all that time, no one had stood up.

No warrior.
No priest.
No king.

So God sent a woman with the heart of a prophet
and the voice of a mother.

Round 6: Deborah — The Fight to Wake the People Up

Her name was Deborah.
And she didn't stand behind a pulpit or atop a warhorse.
She sat beneath a palm tree —
listening, judging, waiting.

The text says she was *leading Israel* —
not with swords,
but with *clarity*.

She wasn't just wise.
She was *anchored*.
A woman of the Word.
A woman of the *whisper*.
A woman who heard God speak… and wasn't afraid to repeat Him.

When Barak hesitated,
she didn't mock his fear.
She simply told him the truth:
"If you won't rise without me, you won't receive the honor."

Not as punishment.
As prophecy.

Because Deborah knew something we forget in times like these:

God doesn't wait forever for someone to say yes.

If you won't rise,
He'll find someone who will.

And the blessing you were meant to carry
might come through someone else's courage.

This isn't about gender.
It's about **availability**.

Round 6: Deborah — The Fight to Wake the People Up

When the ground is shaking
and the enemy is armed
and the people have gone quiet—

God looks for someone
willing to rise.

Deborah didn't ask for applause.
She didn't demand the spotlight.
She *arose* because no one else would.

And through her obedience,
an army was called.
A nation was stirred.
A deliverance was set in motion.

So if you're still waiting on a sign,
still hoping God will send someone else—
maybe this is your palm tree.
Maybe the silence is *your call to speak.*
Maybe this is your moment to rise.

The Rabbi Speaks

Come, student.
Sit with me beneath the palm.

This is not just a tree.
It is a courtroom.
It is a sanctuary.
It is the place where heaven's voice found a willing vessel.

Her name is **Devorah** (דְּבוֹרָה).
It means "bee" — a creature both small and fierce,
capable of sweetness *and* sting,
a builder of hives and protector of queens.

Round 6: Deborah — The Fight to Wake the People Up

Deborah is not a prophet by ambition.
She is a prophet by assignment.

The Hebrew calls her a **nevi'ah** (נְבִיאָה) — a true prophetess —
not one who simply speaks *for* God,
but one who speaks *with His cadence,*
with the gravity of Torah woven into her words.

And she is also called something rarer still:
"A mother in Israel."
Em b'Yisrael (אֵם בְּיִשְׂרָאֵל) — not a title of biology,
but of **spiritual covering**.

She leads not with force,
but with *presence.*
Not from a palace,
but from under a tree between Ramah and Bethel —
two cities whose names mean *"height"* and *"house of God."*

Do you see?
She stands between the mountaintop and the tent of meeting.
Between *calling* and *dwelling.*

And from this place,
she calls Barak.

The message is not hers — it is the Lord's:
"Go. God will draw out the enemy. God will give the victory."

But Barak hesitates.

And here is where we learn the deeper meaning of courage in Hebrew:
It's not the absence of fear.
It's the choice to obey anyway.

Round 6: Deborah — The Fight to Wake the People Up

Deborah does not shame him.
She walks with him.

But she also names the cost of delay:
"The glory will go to another."

In Hebrew, the word for honor is **tiferet** (תִּפְאֶרֶת) — splendor, beauty, dignity.
It is not taken away in judgment.
It simply passes to where obedience flows.

This is not punishment.
It is prophecy.

And now, student, hear this:

Deborah's strength is not in her role.
It is in her *clarity*.
She knows what God has said.
She says it.
And she moves.

In a time when "everyone did what was right in their own eyes,"
she *saw through God's eyes.*
And she became a mirror to a nation that had forgotten how to look upward.

The Rabbi Speaks

Come, student.
Sit with me beneath the palm.

This is not just a tree.
It is a courtroom.
It is a sanctuary.
It is the place where heaven's voice found a willing vessel.

Page | 322

Round 6: Deborah — The Fight to Wake the People Up

Her name is **Devorah** (דְּבוֹרָה).
It means "bee" — a creature both small and fierce,
capable of sweetness *and* sting,
a builder of hives and protector of queens.

Deborah is not a prophet by ambition.
She is a prophet by assignment.

The Hebrew calls her a **nevi'ah** (נְבִיאָה) — a true prophetess —
not one who simply speaks *for* God,
but one who speaks *with His cadence*,
with the gravity of Torah woven into her words.

And she is also called something rarer still:
"A mother in Israel."
Em b'Yisrael (אֵם בְּיִשְׂרָאֵל) — not a title of biology,
but of **spiritual covering**.

She leads not with force,
but with *presence*.
Not from a palace,
but from under a tree between Ramah and Bethel —
two cities whose names mean *"height"* and *"house of God."*

Do you see?
She stands between the mountaintop and the tent of meeting.
Between *calling* and *dwelling*.

And from this place,
she calls Barak.

The message is not hers — it is the Lord's:
"Go. God will draw out the enemy. God will give the victory."

But Barak hesitates.

Round 6: Deborah — The Fight to Wake the People Up

And here is where we learn the deeper meaning of courage in Hebrew:
It's not the absence of fear.
It's the choice to obey anyway.

Deborah does not shame him.
She walks with him.

But she also names the cost of delay:
"The glory will go to another."

In Hebrew, the word for honor is **tiferet** (תִּפְאֶרֶת) — splendor, beauty, dignity.
It is not taken away in judgment.
It simply passes to where obedience flows.

This is not punishment.
It is prophecy.

And now, student, hear this:

Deborah's strength is not in her role.
It is in her *clarity*.
She knows what God has said.
She says it.
And she moves.

In a time when "everyone did what was right in their own eyes,"
she *saw through God's eyes.*
And she became a mirror to a nation that had forgotten how to look upward.

The Fighter Speaks

I didn't ask for this.

I sat beneath a tree
because the people needed someone who would listen —

really listen.
To their disputes.
To their cries.
To the silence between the wars.

They came from every direction,
not because I looked powerful,
but because I didn't flinch.

And when the Word came to me —
not comfort,
not a blessing,
but a *command* —
I knew I couldn't sit any longer.

I called Barak.
Told him what the Lord said.
Told him where to go,
how many to bring,
what mountain to climb.

And he said he'd go…
but only if I did too.

So I went.

Not because I needed to prove anything,
but because he needed someone who wouldn't back down.

I told him the truth:
"A woman will get the glory for this."
Not as a warning.
As a *fact*.

Because when men hesitate,
God doesn't.

He moves through the ones who are willing —
even if they don't look the part.

I never asked for glory.
I asked for *obedience*.
Mine.
His.
Theirs.

I knew who the enemy was.
Not just Sisera.
But fear.
Apathy.
Spiritual amnesia.

The kind that forgets what God has already done
and waits for someone else to act.

So I stood up.

I didn't lift a sword.
But I raised my voice.

And heaven moved.

The Corner Man Speaks

I saw you.

Sitting under the tree when no one else stood.
Holding judgment in one hand and mercy in the other.
Listening while the rest of the world grew numb.

You didn't shout.
You didn't storm the gates.
You just *waited* —
until My voice broke through the silence.

Round 6: Deborah — The Fight to Wake the People Up

And when I spoke,
you didn't second-guess it.
You *acted*.

You called out the fear.
You made room for obedience.
You didn't fight for glory —
you fought for *faithfulness*.

I saw the look in Barak's eyes when you called him.
The hesitation.
The hope.
The need for someone to *go first*.

And you did.

Because that's who you are.
A mother in Israel.
Not because you bore sons,
but because you birthed *courage*.

You rose when others lay low.
You stepped forward when the warriors were unsure.
And through you,
I called a nation back to Me.

Don't think I missed the sacrifice.

You gave up safety for obedience.
You gave up invisibility for leadership.
You gave up comfort for *clarity*.

And I honored it.

Because glory doesn't come to the loudest.
It comes to the *available*.

Round 6: Deborah — The Fight to Wake the People Up

You didn't wait for applause.
You waited for *instruction*.

And when it came,
you said yes.

So now I say this:

Your name will be remembered.
Your song will be sung.
And every time a trembling voice rises in obedience,
your echo will be in it.

Because when you rose…
I did too.

Judges 4:11-16 The Battle Belongs to the Lord

📖 *Judges 4:11–16*

- The armies move—God throws Sisera's forces into panic
- Israel wins, not by might, but by divine confusion
- Barak fights, but only after a woman's word lit the fire
- The Lord routed Sisera—Deborah's prophecy holds true

Judges 4:11–24 (NIV)

Now Heber the Kenite had left the other Kenites, the descendants of Hobab, Moses' brother-in-law,
and pitched his tent by the great tree in Zaanannim near Kedesh.

When they told Sisera that Barak son of Abinoam had gone up to Mount Tabor,
Sisera summoned from Harosheth Haggoyim to the Kishon River all his men and his nine hundred chariots fitted with iron.

Then Deborah said to Barak,
"Go! This is the day the Lord has given Sisera into your hands. Has not the Lord gone ahead of you?"
So Barak went down Mount Tabor, with ten thousand men following him.

At Barak's advance, the Lord routed Sisera and all his chariots and army by the sword,
and Sisera got down from his chariot and fled on foot.

Barak pursued the chariots and army as far as Harosheth Haggoyim,
and all Sisera's troops fell by the sword; not a man was left.

The Preacher Speaks

Round 6: Deborah — The Fight to Wake the People Up

There's a kind of courage that doesn't feel like courage when you're standing in it.

It feels like nausea.
Like dry mouth and cold sweat.
Like staring down a valley filled with metal and men,
and wondering how in the world you got here.

Barak had his orders.
Mount Tabor behind him.
Nine hundred iron chariots ahead.
And somewhere in the middle—his trembling yes to a call he didn't ask for.

That's where faith lives, you know.
Not in the swelling soundtrack of heroism.
But in the quiet moment when someone says,
"Now."

And you have to decide whether you believe that *now* belongs to God, or to the fear gnawing at your ribs.

Deborah speaks like someone who's already seen the battle play out.

She doesn't say,
*"The Lord will go before you."
She says,
"The Lord has gone."

Past tense.
Already done.
Already moving.

That's the kind of theology we don't preach enough.
Not the one that begs for victory,
but the one that believes in a God who *goes ahead.*

Round 6: Deborah — The Fight to Wake the People Up

We forget this sometimes—
that obedience is not about outcome.
It's about alignment.

Barak wasn't told to be brilliant.
He was told to move.

And when he did, something broke open.

The Bible says,
"At Barak's advance, the Lord routed Sisera."

Don't miss that sequence.

The man moved,
and the heavens moved with him.

Sometimes that's all it takes.
Not perfection.
Not bravado.
Just motion in the direction of faith.

And when Sisera fled—on foot, no less,
abandoning his chariot of terror—
you could almost hear the laughter of heaven.

Because when the Lord claims a battle,
He doesn't need better weapons.
He just needs a willing heart.

The Rabbi Speaks

Come, student.
Let us walk the path down from Mount Tabor together.
The wind is shifting.
But it is not only the wind.

There is something in this story that carries the weight of Sinai.

Barak descends with ten thousand men,
but it is the Lord who fights.
The Hebrew says,
"Va'yaham Hashem" (וַיָּהָם יְהוָה) — *"And the Lord threw them into confusion."*

Yaham is not a casual word.
It means to stir, to agitate, to thunder into disorder.
It is used of Pharaoh's army at the Red Sea,
when the wheels of their chariots stuck in the mud and panic filled their lungs.

The sages say that when *yaham* is written,
God Himself is stepping onto the battlefield.

This is not man's victory.
It is *holy disruption*.

Notice, the text does not describe Israel's swords with detail.
It doesn't tell us about military formations or superior strategy.

It tells us only that **"the Lord routed Sisera."**

This is what we call in Hebrew **hashgachah pratit** (הַשְׁגָּחָה פְּרָטִית) —
Divine Providence.
The invisible hand that orchestrates the visible world.

To the Canaanites, it might have looked like a storm.
To the warriors, it might have felt like surprise.
But to the student of Torah,
it is the fingerprint of the One who parts waters,
who topples walls,
who fights for the people He loves.

Round 6: Deborah — The Fight to Wake the People Up

And now look again, student—
at the question Deborah asks:

"Has not the Lord gone ahead of you?"

In Hebrew:
"Halo Yatza Hashem Lifnecha?" (הֲלֹא יָצָא יְהוָה לְפָנֶיךָ)

It is not a rhetorical device.
It is a theology.

Yatza (יָצָא) — to go out, to proceed, to break forth.
And **Lifnecha** (לְפָנֶיךָ) — before you, ahead of you, in front of your face.

She is not asking if Barak believes.
She is reminding him that *he is already following a path God carved in advance.*

This is the gift of faith in Hebrew thinking.
We do not walk into the unknown hoping God will show up.
We walk because **He already has.**

The Fighter Speaks

I saw the chariots gather.
Nine hundred of them.
The sound of iron scraping against earth—
the kind of sound that makes men forget the promises they once believed.

I watched Barak stand there,
his hands full of command,
but his heart still catching up to what God had said.

And I didn't rebuke him.
I didn't question his courage.

Round 6: Deborah — The Fight to Wake the People Up

I just reminded him:
"Has not the Lord already gone ahead?"

Because I knew something fear always forgets—
God doesn't give assignments He won't walk into first.

You think I wasn't afraid too?

I had no sword.
No army.
Just the memory of what God told me beneath that palm tree.

But I knew this:
when the Lord speaks,
He's not predicting the future—
He's *writing it.*

And when He calls you into the fight,
it's because *He's already secured the outcome.*

Barak stepped forward.
And heaven shook the valley.

The battle didn't turn when the swords were drawn.
It turned when faith moved its feet.

We didn't win because we were stronger.
We won because we remembered *who went first.*

That's what I want you to see.

This isn't about confidence.
It's about *clarity.*

And if you have that—
even a sliver of it—
you don't have to wait until you feel brave.

Round 6: Deborah — The Fight to Wake the People Up

You just have to walk forward
like someone who believes the ground has already been claimed by
grace.

Because it has.

The Corner Man Speaks

I saw the fear before you named it.
I watched the chariots gather at the edge of your vision.
And I didn't mock your hesitation.
I didn't call you weak for the way your breath caught at the bottom of
the hill.

Because I know what it feels like
to hear My voice clearly...
and still be afraid to move.

You stood there,
caught between what you believe and what you see—
between My promise
and your pounding heart.

And that's when she turned to you.
Not with a sword.
Not with a plan.
Just with a question wrapped in fire:

"Has not the Lord gone ahead of you?"

She wasn't asking if I would show up.
She was telling you I already had.

I had walked that path before you.
Stepped into that valley long before you put on your armor.

Round 6: Deborah — The Fight to Wake the People Up

I didn't wait for your faith to be perfect.
I moved when your knees were still trembling.

Because that's what covenant looks like.

You don't have to carry certainty.
You just have to carry *Me*.

And when you moved—
when your foot touched the edge of the hill,
and you said yes without knowing how it would end—
I roared through the valley.

Not because you were strong.
But because you *trusted Me enough to move.*

That's all I've ever needed.

One step.

One sliver of faith.
One man who says yes
even while his hands are shaking.

The battle never depended on you.
It never hung on your clarity, your courage, or your credentials.

It belonged to Me.
From the first breath to the final blow.

You saw chariots.
I saw shadows.
You heard the thunder of war.
I heard the rhythm of obedience.

And I will always honor that sound.

Judges 4:17-24 Jael's Tent

📖 *Judges 4:17–24*

- Sisera flees—into the tent of Jael
- She offers him comfort, milk, and a blanket
- Then—like a warrior—she drives the tent peg through his skull
- Deborah had said the glory would go to a woman—but it's not even her
- A foreign woman finishes the enemy with brutal resolve

Judges 4:17–24 (NIV)

Sisera, meanwhile, fled on foot to the tent of Jael, the wife of Heber the Kenite,
because there was an alliance between Jabin king of Hazor and the family of Heber the Kenite.

Jael went out to meet Sisera and said to him,
"Come, my lord, come right in. Don't be afraid."
So he entered her tent, and she covered him with a blanket.

"I'm thirsty," he said. "Please give me some water."
She opened a skin of milk, gave him a drink, and covered him up.

"Stand in the doorway of the tent," he told her.
"If someone comes by and asks you, 'Is anyone in there?' say 'No.'"

But Jael, Heber's wife, picked up a tent peg and a hammer
and went quietly to him while he lay fast asleep, exhausted.
She drove the peg through his temple into the ground, and he died.

Just then Barak came by in pursuit of Sisera,
and Jael went out to meet him. "Come," she said,
"I will show you the man you're looking for."

So he went in with her, and there lay Sisera
with the tent peg through his temple—dead.

On that day God subdued Jabin king of Canaan before the Israelites.
And the hand of the Israelites pressed harder and harder against Jabin
king of Canaan
until they destroyed him.

The Preacher Speaks

Subchapter 3 – Jael's Tent

There are moments in Scripture that feel like they don't belong.

Moments that make us flinch.
Moments that interrupt the narrative we thought we understood.

This is one of them.

The battle was already won.
Sisera had fled.
The thunder of chariots was behind them now.

All that remained was a single man running for his life—
a commander without an army,
a tyrant without his throne.

And where does he run?

To a quiet tent.
To a woman who should've been an ally.

Her name is Jael.

She offers him shelter.
A blanket.
Warm milk.
Words that sound like safety.

Round 6: Deborah — The Fight to Wake the People Up

And then—
silence breaks into judgment.

A tent peg.
A hammer.
A blow that ends a legacy of violence in the stillness of a stranger's dwelling.

It's shocking.
Undeniably so.

But Scripture doesn't apologize for it.

Because Jael wasn't acting out of rage.
She wasn't hunting glory.
She was ending a war.

We don't know all her reasons.
We don't need to.

We just know that her actions—however brutal they may seem to us—
were the final thread in a tapestry God had been weaving since the first
verse of the chapter.

It was Deborah who prophesied it,
long before the tent or the blanket or the milk:

"The Lord will deliver Sisera into the hands of a woman."

And He did.

Not in the way Barak expected.
Not in the way we might prefer.

But in the way that revealed, yet again,
that God chooses the unexpected
to dismantle the unbearable.

The battle did not end with a trumpet blast.
It ended with a whisper… and a hammer.

And maybe that's the point.

Sometimes, God's justice doesn't march through the front gate.
It sneaks in the side door
and waits until the oppressor has fallen asleep.

The Rabbi Speaks

Then come, student.

Take off your sandals as you enter the tent—
not out of fear,
but reverence.

Because the Rabbi is here.
And what looks to us like violence or surprise…
he sees as layers of *chesed*, *teshuvah*, and truth.

This is not a story for the faint of heart—
but neither is it one to be dismissed as mere brutality.

This is Torah.

And Torah does not hide its difficult moments.
It weaves them.

You ask, *"Why would God allow such an ending?"*
Let us begin not with answers—
but with names.

Yael (יָעֵל).
Her name means "mountain goat."
A creature that walks dangerous terrain with quiet strength.
She does not storm the battlefield.

Round 6: Deborah — The Fight to Wake the People Up

She waits on the edge of it.
And when the moment comes, she moves without fanfare.

Notice what she offers:

- A blanket.

- Milk instead of water.

- Reassurance, not resistance.

Every one of these is a layer of disarming.
Not deceit for gain—
but preparation for justice.

And now remember the prophecy:

"The honor will not be yours, Barak, for the Lord will deliver Sisera into the hands of a woman."

That woman is not Deborah.
It is Yael.

Why?

Because in Hebrew thinking, justice is not only about *who fights*.
It is about *who finishes*.

God does not just defeat evil.
He *disarms it*.

And when Sisera falls asleep under Yael's roof—
covered, fed, secure—
he has no idea that he has already entered judgment.

There is a Hebrew concept here, one we must not forget:

midah k'neged midah (מידה כנגד מידה) —
measure for measure.

Sisera's life was marked by terror.
Oppression.
Domination of the vulnerable.

And now—
at the hands of one who had every reason to remain silent—
his reign ends not with an army,
but with a single, decisive act of divine reckoning.

Is it uncomfortable? Yes.
But so is any surgery that saves a life.

This tent is not a courtroom.
But it is a place of justice.

Because when God promises deliverance,
He does not always send chariots.
Sometimes, He sends milk.
And a woman with steady hands.

The Fighter Speaks

Subchapter 3 – Jael's Tent

I wasn't part of the plan.
No prophecy named me.
No general called me forward.
I wasn't a soldier or a judge—
just a woman with a tent…
and eyes that had seen enough.

Round 6: Deborah — The Fight to Wake the People Up

He came into my home like I owed him silence.
Like I was an extension of his retreat.
Like peace meant pretending I didn't know what he had done.

But I knew.

I knew the stories.
What he did to women in the towns he conquered.
What his chariots left behind.
I knew what it meant when a tyrant asked for water but expected milk.

So I gave him what he wanted—
softness.
Safety.
Sleep.

Then I gave him what God wanted—
an end.

I didn't do it for glory.
I didn't do it to make history.
I did it because no one else was in the tent.
And I was done waiting for someone stronger to show up.

They'll talk about Deborah.
They'll remember Barak.
But I want you to remember me, too.

Not because of what I did—
but because of what I saw:

That the enemy can look tired.
He can look pitiful.
He can even look like a guest.

But if you let him rest in your house,
he'll rise again with a sword.

So I didn't let him rise.

I drove truth through the lies
and pinned them to the ground.

And when Barak showed up,
still chasing the man I'd already buried,
I didn't boast.
I didn't gloat.

I just opened the tent
and showed him what it looks like
when obedience wears earrings
instead of armor.

The Corner Man Speaks

Subchapter 3 – Jael's Tent

They didn't invite you to the war.
Didn't ask for your help.
Didn't imagine that deliverance could come through hands like yours.

But I knew.

While they counted swords and chariots,
I was watching your tent.
While they planned their charge,
I was listening for the sound of your courage waking up.

And when he ran—
when he crossed the line and came into your house,
smiling with fear disguised as entitlement—
I leaned in.

Round 6: Deborah — The Fight to Wake the People Up

Because this was your round.

You didn't have an army.
You didn't have a prophecy written in your name.
But you had something else.

You had enough.

Enough of the lies.
Enough of the violence.
Enough of the silence that too often protects the wrong people.

And you said yes.

You said yes with a blanket.
Yes with a bottle of milk.
Yes with a hammer in your hand
and My strength in your spine.

Don't let anyone tell you it was too much.
Don't let them rewrite what I have already recorded.

I didn't flinch.
I didn't turn away.
I saw you move with holy precision.

Because sometimes righteousness doesn't come in robes—
it comes in calloused hands,
driven by conviction,
guided by My justice.

You didn't need permission.
You needed presence.

And I was with you.
Every breath.

Round 6: Deborah — The Fight to Wake the People Up

Every step.
Every strike.

What you did was not vengeance.
It was faith.

Because when the enemy came into your tent,
you didn't invite him to stay.
You drove him out the only way he could be stopped.

And I will tell your story.
Not just in Judges—
but in the lives of those who feel invisible,
overlooked,
too late to the battle.

Because I don't just bless the bold who lead the charge.
I bless the ones who finish it
when no one else had the courage to do so.

Judges 5:1-31 The Song of Deborah

📖 *Judges 5:1–31*

- A prophetic poem, sung in the aftermath
- It names the warriors, praises the willing, and rebukes the complacent
- "Wake up, Deborah... Rise up, Barak..." — this was never just about war
- The land has rest for forty years—but Deborah's voice still echoes for those who sleep in fear and silence

Judges 5:1–31 (NIV)

On that day Deborah and Barak son of Abinoam sang this song:

"When the princes in Israel take the lead,
when the people willingly offer themselves—
praise the Lord!

"Hear this, you kings! Listen, you rulers!
I, even I, will sing to the Lord;
I will praise the Lord, the God of Israel, in song.

"When you, Lord, went out from Seir,
when you marched from the land of Edom,
the earth shook, the heavens poured,
the clouds poured down water.

The mountains quaked before the Lord, the One of Sinai,
before the Lord, the God of Israel.

"In the days of Shamgar son of Anath,
in the days of Jael, the highways were abandoned;
travelers took to winding paths.

Round 6: Deborah — The Fight to Wake the People Up

Villagers in Israel would not fight;
they held back until I, Deborah, arose,
until I arose, a mother in Israel.

God chose new leaders
when war came to the city gates,
but not a shield or spear was seen
among forty thousand in Israel.

My heart is with Israel's princes,
with the willing volunteers among the people.
Praise the Lord!

"You who ride on white donkeys,
sitting on your saddle blankets,
and you who walk along the road, consider

the voice of the singers at the watering places.
They recite the victories of the Lord,
the victories of his villagers in Israel.

"Then the people of the Lord
went down to the city gates.
'Wake up, wake up, Deborah!
Wake up, wake up, break out in song!
Arise, Barak!
Take captive your captives, son of Abinoam.'

"The remnant of the nobles came down;
the people of the Lord came down to me against the mighty.

Some came from Ephraim, whose roots were in Amalek;
Benjamin was with the people who followed you.
From Makir captains came down,
from Zebulun those who bear a commander's staff.

Round 6: Deborah — The Fight to Wake the People Up

The princes of Issachar were with Deborah;
yes, Issachar was with Barak,
sent under his command into the valley.

In the districts of Reuben
there was much searching of heart.

Why did you stay among the sheep pens
to hear the whistling for the flocks?
In the districts of Reuben
there was much searching of heart.

Gilead stayed beyond the Jordan.
And Dan—why did he linger by the ships?
Asher remained on the coast
and stayed in his coves.

The people of Zebulun risked their very lives;
so did Naphtali on the terraced fields.

"Kings came, they fought,
the kings of Canaan fought.
At Taanach, by the waters of Megiddo,
they took no plunder of silver.

From the heavens the stars fought,
from their courses they fought against Sisera.

The river Kishon swept them away,
the age-old river, the river Kishon.
March on, my soul; be strong!

Then thundered the horses' hooves—
galloping, galloping go his mighty steeds.

'Curse Meroz,' said the angel of the Lord.
'Curse its people bitterly,

because they did not come to help the Lord,
to help the Lord against the mighty.'

"Most blessed of women be Jael,
the wife of Heber the Kenite,
most blessed of tent-dwelling women.

He asked for water, and she gave him milk;
in a bowl fit for nobles she brought him curdled milk.

Her hand reached for the tent peg,
her right hand for the workman's hammer.
She struck Sisera, she crushed his head,
she shattered and pierced his temple.

At her feet he sank, he fell;
there he lay.
At her feet he sank, he fell;
where he sank, there he fell—dead.

"Through the window peered Sisera's mother;
behind the lattice she cried out,
'Why is his chariot so long in coming?
Why is the clatter of his chariots delayed?'

The wisest of her ladies answer her;
indeed, she keeps saying to herself,

'Are they not finding and dividing the spoils:
a woman or two for each man,
colorful garments as plunder for Sisera,
colorful garments embroidered,
highly embroidered garments for my neck—
all this as plunder?'

Round 6: Deborah — The Fight to Wake the People Up

"So may all your enemies perish, Lord!
But may all who love you be like the sun
when it rises in its strength."

Then the land had peace forty years.

The Preacher Speaks

Some stories are too holy to be told in prose.
They demand music.

And this—this is one of them.

Deborah doesn't just recount the battle.
She *sings it*.
Because some victories aren't complete until they're *remembered out loud*.

This song is not about strategy.
It's about *availability*.
It names the tribes who showed up…
and the ones who stayed home.

Zebulun and Naphtali risked their lives.
Reuben "searched his heart," but never left the pasture.
Dan lingered with his ships.
Asher stayed by the sea.

God wasn't looking for the strongest.
He was looking for the willing.

And in the center of it all—
a mother in Israel, rising up.
Not because she wanted fame,
but because no one else was standing.

This isn't the song of a general.
It's the cry of a prophet

who saw God move in thunder, stars, and rivers…
but also in volunteers, in risk, and in tents.

Even the heavens fought that day.
The stars themselves joined the battle.

And as the dust settled,
Deborah remembered Jael.

Not as a footnote.
Not as an exception.
But as *the most blessed of women.*

Because she didn't flinch when evil knocked on her door.
She didn't wait for permission to act.
She saw the moment—and she stepped into it.

Even Sisera's mother makes it into the song.
Waiting by the window…
dreaming of embroidered garments…
while her son lies dead under a borrowed blanket.

The whole song ends with this:

"May all who love You be like the sun when it rises in its strength."

That's not sentiment.
It's a *commission.*

Because when we show up—when we move at God's whisper,
when we act in courage instead of fear—
we don't just witness the sunrise…

We *become* it.

The Rabbi Speaks

Round 6: Deborah — The Fight to Wake the People Up

You've heard the melody.
Now listen for the meaning.

This is not merely a victory hymn.
It is a *midrash in music*—
a sacred unpacking of what just took place.

In Hebrew thought, songs are more than celebration.
They are *preservation*.
A way of binding memory to rhythm
so that the next generation will not forget what God has done.

So Deborah sings.

But notice—this is not a solo.

She sings **with Barak**.
The one who once hesitated now lends his voice to remembrance.
Because sometimes the most courageous thing a man can do
is join a woman's song.

The structure is layered like Torah itself.

It opens with praise—
"When the leaders lead, and the people volunteer—bless the Lord!"
It remembers how God moved—
thunder shaking the mountains, rivers rising against the enemy.
It recalls the vulnerability of Israel—
no shields, no spears, no roads.

And then comes the *naming*.

Those who stepped forward:
Zebulun. Naphtali. Ephraim. Benjamin. Issachar.

Round 6: Deborah — The Fight to Wake the People Up

And those who stayed behind:
Reuben. Dan. Asher. Gilead.

The song does not shame—
but it *remembers truthfully*.

Because faith is not abstract in Israel.
It is always embodied.
Who showed up? Who didn't?
These questions matter.

And then—
Yael.

The song lifts her not as a footnote,
but as the fulcrum.
The axis around which the victory turns.

She is called **"most blessed of women"**—
a phrase echoed later for only one other: *Mary of Nazareth*.

Why?

Because she did what needed doing
when no one else would do it.

And at the close, we hear a mother—
not Deborah this time,
but Sisera's mother—
peering through the lattice,
dreaming of embroidered spoils and captive women.

Her silence becomes a final contrast.
The song ends not with her grief,
but with this benediction:

"May all who love You be like the sun when it rises in its strength."

In Hebrew, the sun is more than light.
It is *faithfulness*.
It rises every morning without fail.
It gives life without needing applause.

So too is the one who walks in God's way.

Rise, student.
Rise like that sun.

You are not just meant to survive your battles.
You are meant to *remember them in song*.

Let me know when you're ready for the Fighter.
She remembers too—
not with theology or melody,
but with that sharp, sacred edge of someone who lived it.

The Fighter Speaks

Subchapter 4 – The Song of Deborah

They wrote it into a song.

What I lived—
what I bled for—
they turned into poetry.

And I didn't mind.

Because this time…
they remembered.

They remembered who showed up.
Who stepped into the fight.
Who watched the odds tilt like iron chariots in the sun—
and moved anyway.

They remembered who stayed home too.
And that mattered.
Because silence is part of the story,
even when it doesn't make a sound.

I was there when it happened—
when the heavens joined us,
when rivers rose like warriors,
when fear broke open and became faith.

I felt the ground move.
Not just under Sisera's hooves,
but under *ours*—
when we stopped waiting to be rescued
and started moving like we already were.

You want to know the truth?

That song wasn't just about us.
It was *for* the ones who'd come after.
The ones who don't feel strong.
The ones who hesitate.
The ones who've been told they're too late, too little, too ordinary.

The song is their reminder.

That when God fights,
He doesn't just use swords.
He uses singers.
He uses tents.
He uses the ones who show up when others stay behind.

Round 6: Deborah — The Fight to Wake the People Up

So yeah… they wrote a song.

And I hope it echoes
every time someone stands up shaking
but doesn't sit back down.

Because that's all we did.

We showed up.
We risked something.
We let the sun rise inside us.

And somehow, that was enough
to bring peace to the land
for forty years.

The Corner Man Speaks

Subchapter 4 – The Song of Deborah

I saw who stepped forward.
And I saw who stayed behind.

I didn't need the song to remind Me—
I never forget the ones who move when it's hard.

You thought no one noticed
when you left the pasture,
when you put your foot in the valley,
when you stood beside someone braver than you and borrowed their
courage.

But I saw it.

I saw you when you weren't the strongest,
weren't the loudest,
weren't the first.

Round 6: Deborah — The Fight to Wake the People Up

I saw you show up anyway.

And that matters more than you know.

Because I'm not counting victories.
I'm counting *volunteers*.

Not just the ones who carried weapons—
but the ones who carried *hope*.
The ones who didn't wait for certainty,
who didn't hide behind strategy,
who heard the call and moved.

There's a reason the song names every tribe.
Even the ones who stayed.
Even the ones who searched their hearts but never left the shoreline.

Because this isn't just a record of war.
It's a mirror.
And I want you to see yourself in it.

You don't have to be Deborah.
You don't have to be Jael.

You just have to show up when I call.

And when you do—
even trembling,
even late,
even unsure—
I will make your presence feel like sunrise.

Because when you walk with Me,
your obedience becomes brightness.
Your risk becomes rhythm.
Your story becomes song.

Round 6: Deborah — The Fight to Wake the People Up

You won't always make the front lines.
You won't always get the credit.

But I'll write you in.

Right there, between the rivers and the thunder.

Because I remember the ones who moved.
And I bless the ones who still do.

In This Corner: Deborah – Round 6
You didn't ask for the spotlight.
You didn't wake up wanting to be brave.
You just saw the moment… and stepped into it.

That's what Deborah did.

She didn't plan a war.
She didn't beg for power.
She simply *rose*—
a mother in Israel
who saw that no one else was leading,
and decided silence wasn't an option.

Barak hesitated.
She didn't shame him.
She went with him.

Because sometimes leadership doesn't look like control.
It looks like *companionship.*

Sometimes the bravest thing you can do
is sing your faith until someone else believes it too.

And Jael?
She wasn't in the prophecy.
She wasn't invited to the front lines.
But she refused to let evil rest in her house.

You think you need a sword to make a difference.
But maybe all you need is **presence.**
The kind that wraps truth in a blanket
and ends what everyone else was afraid to finish.

And don't miss this:
God told their story in a song.

Round 6: Deborah — The Fight to Wake the People Up

Not just a victory report—
a **melody of memory**.

Because when you fight with faith,
even your footsteps get written in harmony.

Deborah's blessing didn't come from ease.
It came from *endurance*.
From leading when she wasn't asked to.
From singing when others stayed silent.
From standing when everything said to sit down.

So what about you?

Maybe you're not the loudest.
Maybe you're not the first.
Maybe the ones you counted on stayed behind.

But if you're still here…
still rising,
still showing up with trembling hands and a heart full of questions…

Then this is your round.

And I promise—
you don't have to feel strong
to be used mightily.

Because the God of Deborah is still moving.
Still shaking the heavens.
Still writing songs.

And He's not done singing *your* story.

Epilogue

"The Bell Never Meant You Lost"
Maybe you made it here bloodied and breathless.
Maybe you didn't expect to last this long.
Maybe you thought by now the struggle would be over—but it's not.

You've come through six rounds.
Each one a story that left marks.
Not just on the characters—but on you.

You wrestled through the night with **Jacob**,
refusing to let go until the blessing came.
You stood beneath the stars with **Abraham**,
bargaining for mercy, holding God to His own name.
You argued with **Moses**, barefoot before the burning bush,
wondering if calling and fear could ever live in the same heart.
You sat with **Job** in the ash heap,
where silence screamed louder than answers.
You followed **Ruth** into fields of rejection and risk,
offering covenantal love even when no one asked for it.
And you stood beside **Deborah**,
on a hilltop between fear and faith,
learning that courage doesn't always come with clarity.

Maybe, in their stories, you started to see your own.
Not because you share their culture or time,
but because you share their condition:
You are someone who has dared to wrestle with God and not let go.

Epilogue

The truth is, we don't get to choose whether we wrestle.
Life brings the fight to us.
We only choose whether we stay in the ring.

And if you're still here—still reading, still reaching, still refusing to tap out—
Then hear this again:

You are not losing.
You are not behind.
You are not broken because you're tired.

You are in the fight.
And that means you're exactly where you're supposed to be.

The bell ringing at the end of this match?
It's not a signal of defeat.
It's a breath between battles.

Because there's more ahead.
More stories.
More voices.
More rounds.

And the same God who met **Jacob** in the dark,
who bargained with **Abraham**,
who called **Moses** through trembling,
who listened to **Job's** rage,
who honored **Ruth's** loyalty,
and who spoke through **Deborah's** strength—
That God is still in your corner.

Epilogue

You may be limping, but you're not disqualified.
You may be doubting, but you're not dismissed.
You may be swinging wild, but you're still held.

So take a moment here.
Exhale.
Tend to the bruises.
Remember the blessing.

But the fight isn't over.

What began with Jacob's limp and Job's lament now stretches into new arenas—sanctuaries, palaces, caves, and crosses. In *Match Two: The Fire, the Silence, and the Surrender*, we step into the ring with those who battled from the margins and the throne rooms, the wilderness and the womb. Hannah will fight to be heard. Elijah will burn out after the fire. David will fall and still chase after God's heart. Esther will risk everything in silence. Jonah will run from mercy. And Jesus… Jesus will sweat blood in the garden and rise from the grave with scars still showing.

Each story will ask you to wrestle again—not just with God, but with what it means to trust Him when the blessing costs more than you expected.

The bell will ring again.

Will you step in?

Glossary of Hebraic and Rabbinic Terms

This glossary offers definitions and insights into key terms featured in the Rabbi's commentary, aiding readers in navigating the rich tapestry of Jewish thought and tradition.

Aggadah (אַגָּדָה)

Literal Meaning: Narrative or tale. Used In: Non-legalistic teachings and moral stories. Insight: Aggadah comprises the narrative aspects of rabbinic literature, offering ethical insights, theological concepts, and cultural values through storytelling.

Am ha'aretz (עַם הָאָרֶץ)

Literal Meaning: People of the land. Used In: References to common folk or those less versed in religious law. Insight: Historically, am ha'aretz referred to Jews who were not meticulous in religious observance, highlighting tensions between scholarly elites and the general populace.

Chazal (חכמינו זיכרונם לברכה)

Literal Meaning: "Our sages, may their memory be a blessing." Used In: Rabbinic commentary and interpretive traditions. Insight: Chazal refers collectively to the rabbis of the Mishnah, Talmud, and Midrash—spiritual ancestors whose teachings shape the core of Jewish thought.

Chesed (חֶסֶד)

Literal Meaning: Lovingkindness, covenant faithfulness. Used In: Ruth's vow to Naomi and as a core concept in divine-human relationships. Insight: Chesed reflects a kind of love that is steadfast and loyal even when undeserved. It's not mere affection—it is love tied to covenant, mercy, and sacrifice.

Chokhmah (חָכְמָה)

Literal Meaning: Wisdom. Used In: Discussions on knowledge, understanding, and insight. Insight: Chokhmah signifies not just intellectual acumen but a profound, often spiritual, wisdom that guides ethical and moral decision-making.

Gibor (גִּבּוֹר)

Literal Meaning: Mighty one, warrior. Used In: Descriptions of Deborah's courage and Jael's strength. Insight: Not gender-specific. Used of anyone whose courage serves divine justice.

Halakhah (הֲלָכָה)

Literal Meaning: The way or path. Used In: Legal rulings and religious observances. Insight: Halakhah refers to the collective body of Jewish law, encompassing commandments, customs, and traditions that dictate daily life and spiritual practice.

Midrash (מִדְרָשׁ)

Literal Meaning: Inquiry or interpretation. Used In: Analytical discussions and explorations of biblical texts. Insight: Midrash represents a method of interpreting scriptures that seeks deeper meanings, often revealing moral and spiritual lessons beyond the literal text.

Mishpat (מִשְׁפָּט)

Literal Meaning: Judgment or legal decision. Used In: Contexts involving law, justice, and societal order. Insight: Mishpat underscores the importance of a just legal system, emphasizing fairness and the rule of law as foundational to communal life.

Moab (מוֹאָב)

Literal Meaning: From father. Used In: Background of Ruth's ancestry. Insight: Originates from the story of Lot's daughter. The name itself carries cultural and moral stigma in ancient Israel, making Ruth's story a radical reversal.

Ruach (רוּחַ)

Literal Meaning: Spirit, wind, breath. Used In: Descriptions of divine movement or inner strength. Insight: Ruach is used throughout the Tanakh to signify God's spirit, creative breath, or the animating force in humanity.

Shema (שְׁמַע)

Literal Meaning: Hear or listen. Used In: Central declarations of faith and monotheism. Insight: The Shema is a foundational Jewish prayer affirming the oneness of God, encapsulating the essence of Jewish belief and devotion.

Shevet (שֵׁבֶט)

Literal Meaning: Tribe or staff. Used In: Song of Deborah listing which tribes responded. Insight: Often denotes not just bloodline but symbolic authority and alignment in divine movements.

Shuv (שׁוּב)

Literal Meaning: To turn or return. Used In: Rabbi's commentary on repeated use in Ruth 1. Insight: Shuv is the root word of teshuvah and emphasizes the act of turning around—both physically and spiritually.

Talmud (תַּלְמוּד)

Literal Meaning: Study or learning. Used In: Discussions involving Jewish law, ethics, and tradition. Insight: The Talmud is a central text in Judaism, comprising rabbinical discussions and interpretations that guide religious practice and ethical conduct.

Teshuvah (תְּשׁוּבָה)

Literal Meaning: Return, repentance. Used In: Naomi's return to Bethlehem; a spiritual journey as much as a geographical one. Insight: In Hebrew thought, teshuvah is a turning of the heart toward God. It's central to transformation, not just morally, but relationally.

Tzedakah (צְדָקָה)

Literal Meaning: Righteousness or justice. Used In: Discussions on ethical obligations and charitable acts. Insight: Beyond mere charity, tzedakah embodies a moral duty to pursue justice and equity, reflecting a core principle in Jewish ethics.

Yashar (יָשָׁר)

Literal Meaning: Upright, straight. Used In: In reference to Jacob's transformation into Israel. Insight: The name Israel (יִשְׂרָאֵל) contains this root, meaning "one who wrestles with God" but also connoting righteousness through struggle.

www.ingramcontent.com/pod-product-compliance
Lightning Source LLC
Chambersburg PA
CBHW070546130626
46556CB00001B/30